Simple Expressions

Creative and Therapeutic Arts for the Elderly in Long-Term Care Facilities

by

Vicki Parsons

Illustrated by Gregory M. Parsons

Venture Publishing, Inc.
1999 Cato Avenue
State College, PA 16801

Production Manager: Richard Yocum
Manuscript Editing and Design: Michele L. Barbin
Additional Editing: Matthew S. Weaver
Cover Design and Artwork: ©1998 Sandra Sikorski

Library of Congress Catalogue Card Number 98-84476
ISBN 0-910251-97-5

This book is dedicated to my three wonderful children.
Gregory's creative expression brings life to
a drawing or a piece of music.
Melissa moves to music expressing herself through dance.
Brian *is* expression!

Contents

Chapter 4
Crayon Expressions *39*

Chapter 5
Clay Expressions *47*

Clay Recipes...

...and Expressions

Chapter 6
Crafty Expressions *59*

Collage Expressions

Chapter 7
Nature Expressions *89*

Preface

This book was written in response to the many frustrated activity and recreation professionals I have consulted with or taught in the past several years. I witnessed too many activity directors standing along the sidelines or sitting in an office instead of being in the middle of an activity with their residents. I also have tremendous success in carrying out these "simple expressions" with the institutionalized elderly. Although this book is written with residents in long-term care facilities in mind, the activities are appropriate for use in adult day-care centers, continuing care residence centers, and assisted living facilities.

Activity professionals working in nursing facilities, adult day-care facilities and other long-term care facilities for the elderly are charged with providing activities which either support, maintain or empower the older adults with whom they work. Activity professionals need to meet the individual needs of each client by providing opportunities for group and independent activities. This is difficult even under the best conditions. Activity and recreation staff in long-term care facilities must balance the time they spend with the residents with the time they spend on required documentation.

I have observed activity professionals running on a treadmill that they can't get off. The pressure of completing paperwork begins to squeeze out any time he or she has to develop his or her own creative ideas, much less that of the residents. It becomes easier to continue doing what has always been done, or to pay for expensive supplies, equipment or extra staff, than to take the time to think of new directions in which take their programs. Innovative directions provide meaningful leisure-time activities for the people they serve.

Many facilities are seeing more and more older adults who have been diagnosed with some form of dementia. These residents are not always capable of fitting into the traditional routine found within many activity departments. Activity and recreation staff are frustrated because the "normal," everyday activities just don't work anymore.

Now is the time for activity and recreation directors to get back to the basics—back to really being with their residents. It is time to go beyond what is seen as "normal" for activities. Activity service professionals must "unblock their imaginations." I once heard a story about a naturalist who was studying the processionary caterpillar. Several of these caterpillars were placed on the rim of a large, clay flowerpot. Food was placed down inside the flowerpot. The naturalist watched them. For seven days (a long time in the life of a caterpillar) they just followed each other around and around the rim of the flower pot. They never went down into the flowerpot to get food. They never took a new direction. They traditionally followed each other around the rim. It's what they always did! Certainly, I am not making too close a comparison between the processionary caterpillar and the activity professional, but I suspect there are many professionals who follow what has always been done. Yes, it's easier. It may even be safer. But it's time to find a new direction and venture off the rim!

There will be some who look at the ideas in this book and immediately deny their residents' interest or ability. For those people, there is a Chinese proverb that says, "Man who say it cannot be done should not interrupt man who is doing it."

I hope that you will take advantage of the activities in this book. More importantly I hope that you understand the concept behind *Simple Expressions*: Take the time to be with your residents. Touch them, sing with them, play with them, and laugh with them. Be spontaneous, seize the moment, be spirited—and be optimistic!

The author and publisher caution the professional to be sensitive to the abilities and limitations of your participants. The nature of some activities may not be appropriate for your clients. Professional judgment on your part is required.

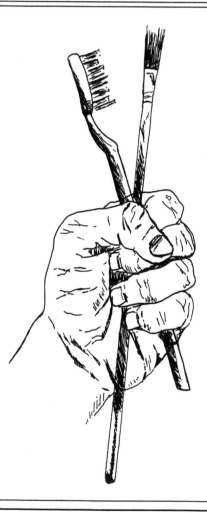

Chapter 1

Introduction

The activities offered in nursing homes are, many times, activities that require a start and a finish with specific steps in between. There is nothing wrong with these activities, and activities departments should certainly offer them, but very often the steps become tedious, or even too difficult for the resident struggling with his or her small motor skills or attention span. Then there are the residents who may be confused or disoriented and are unable to follow the instructions necessary to complete the activity.

Question whether these structured activities really offer opportunity for "creative expression." Are we too often looking for a product? Or something that can be displayed in a showcase? Or sold at a craft bazaar? There is nothing wrong with doing this; there are definitely some benefits to residents with these kinds of activities. However, there are many people who need to be able to stroke just one color of paint across a piece of paper, squeeze some clay, throw newspaper balls across a room, paint a rock or sculpt with marshmallows, and have that be OK. Challenge yourself to consider that it is the *process,* not the *product,* which might be most beneficial to your residents. In fact, the process is *the* thing you are interested in when you are working in any developmental, educational or therapeutic setting. A resident with Alzheimer's disease may have a craft decorating his or her room that he or she made with the help of the activity coordinator, recreation director or volunteer, but chances are, he or she cannot remember that *he* or *she* made the craft. It is also very possible that the *process* of putting together the craft was not done by the resident. Remember, the process is more important than the product! Further remember, it is *the* one thing you should be most interested in when it comes to providing activity services for your clients. The wonderful thing about working with residents with dementia is that you can do these activities every day. They are new to the resident with dementia each time you do them.

Your goal is *not* to create a professional "artist" or "actor." Your goal is to offer an opportunity for the residents to express themselves through art or thought. Your goal is to help develop or maintain happy, creative individuals who feel good about themselves and their abilities. There is no "right" or "wrong" when working with creative expression. Be careful that the facilitator presents the ideas in a non-threatening way. Don't push styles on another individual. There is no correct design for finished pieces. And although there *may* be a "correct" answer for the activities in chapter 10, Expressions of Thought, it is the thinking and wondering that gives the resident the greatest benefit. These activities are simply a time for self-expression—simple expressions.

The activity or recreation director may have to drop old habits. Eliminate "good," "bad," "right," and other value judgments relating to products. Use phrases like, "I like the colors you chose to use," "You worked hard to create with your clay," or "You put a lot of thought into that." You definitely want to stay away from phrases like, "What is it?" and "I can't tell what it looks like," and "That's not the right answer."

As the facilitator, be determined to always be positive, enthusiastic and spontaneous in your approach. Go into each activity thinking that your residents will *really love* what you're about to do—and keep thinking that way! Your positive approach will create an attitude of confidence and will encourage creativity in everyone.

Creative arts can be anything that allows for creativity! Colors, movement, mime, storytelling, drama, props, music and thinking are a few essentials as you'll see in the rest of this book. The activities in this book are inexpensive, yet they are priceless in their benefits. The fun and laughter will be some of the best therapy you offer! Probably even for you—the activity director.

Other benefits of providing expressive and creative arts for the elderly are the opportunities for self-expression, for developing confidence in oneself, to explore and think, to embrace imagination, to socialize and communicate with other residents, for emotional outlets, and it just adds pizzazz to the residents' daily life!

Creative art can be defined as "the mirror of one's creative energy." Used as a therapy, creative art does not have to be aesthetically beautiful. It just needs to provide an opportunity for expression.

Keep the sessions short. A half-hour is usually an adequate amount of time, but keep in mind that some people may only spend five minutes participating. Recognize your residents' limitations. Don't worry if you have a resident who paints, then wanders away for a few minutes. Remember that attention spans vary. The ideal would be to have a variety of these activities set up during the day so that your residents *can* wander in and out and take part when they desire. This may not always be practical, especially when there is a limited activity staff, but maybe this will be an incentive to develop a better volunteer program!

Most of the following ideas in this book are just "simple expressions." There is nothing difficult about them. There are a few ideas to help you develop the "creative expression" idea and take it to higher levels as well. Experiment a little yourself! Try out new materials and mediums to see how they will work. Most of all, have fun!

Chapter 2
Supplies

You may not have any of these supplies at this time, but don't run out and buy everything either. Remember, try to keep from spending a lot of money. Most of these supplies can be purchased over a period of time; many can be donated; and of course, garage sales are *great!* When collecting supplies, look at *everything* with a creative eye. Ask yourself the question, "Could I use this in an activity with the residents?" Many of these supplies can be found for free just by looking around or asking.

Here are some suggestions for supplies to start gathering for your programs. For art supplies check local craft, hobby and school supply stores. *Be sure to take precautions with every activity if any of the residents have a tendency to place things in his or her mouth.*

A warming tray
Iron
Toaster oven
Hot glue gun
Tape recorder
Sponges
Paint brushes (various sizes)
Butcher paper
Resealable, plastic bags (sandwich-size and gallon-size)
Empty roll-on deodorant containers
Squeeze bottles (such as those used for ketchup and mustard)

Spray bottles (such as those used for plants or
   household cleaners; ones with adjustable
   nozzles are best)
Wallpaper sample books
Carpet samples
White glue
Liquid starch
Tempera paint (powdered and liquid)
Watercolor paint
Food coloring
Crayons (new and old, broken ones)
Chalk (various widths; sidewalk chalk is easi-
   est for some residents to hold)
Markers (nontoxic, overhead and permanent)
Finger-paint paper
Construction paper
Manila paper
Poster board
Cardboard
Wax paper
Cloth/Material
An easel or two
Chenille stems (found in craft stores)
Magnets
Sand
Disposable latex gloves for the residents (only use
when necessary)
Smocks or aprons (smocks can be old oversized
   shirts that someone donated)

Many things can be added to these basic supplies—buttons,
shells, feathers, cotton, sand, or anything else that can be
incorporated into a piece of artwork. Let your imagination
guide you.

Keep a good supply of large plastic garbage bags and
newspapers to cover tabletops and the floor when necessary. Thin shower curtains, which are inexpensive and reusable, work very well. When the activity is over the
shower curtains can be wiped off, thrown in a washing machine, or hosed off outside.

A piece of yarn or clothesline strung across a room and clothespins can be used to pin up painted paper that needs to dry.

Often there will be beautiful paintings that you will want to display (even though it is the *process* and not the product that is important). Inquire at framing shops, art galleries and craft stores to see if they will donate unused matting in various sizes. "Imitation" matting can also be made from poster board or construction paper. There's just something about framing a painting that really shows it off.

Have people collect old hats, scarves and other articles of clothing that could be used in some of the theater arts activities. Visit a Goodwill store or a thrift shop and you may find what you need. Don't feel you need to collect everything at once.

Recipes can be found in chapters three and five for making homemade paints and clays.

Chapter 3

Paint Expressions

Painting can be done with just about anything from feathers and sponges to fingers and brushes. Even painting with a brush can take on many different forms. A paintbrush can be tapped, twisted, pressed, brushed, and so on—each creating a different effect. Look over your "throwaways"—you can use them for some paint expressions. Eyedroppers, empty plastic squeeze bottles, spray bottles, even plastic medicine cups can be dipped in paint to make circular designs on paper.

Invest in materials that will meet your needs, but consider the quality you want. For instance, watercolors can be purchased in a tray similar to the kind we send to school with children. These watercolor trays are inexpensive, but they will not give you the results that watercolors from tubes with much more brilliant colors will. Paper quality should also be considered. If you are using a thinned tempera paint or watercolors, thin paper like newsprint may tear. A higher quality, more absorbent paper can be purchased for a little more money, and it will give you far better results. Take good care of reusable supplies such as paintbrushes. Be sure all reusable supplies are thoroughly cleaned and carefully stored between uses.

For painting activities involving brushes, supply enough brushes so that there are one or two brushes for each color, or place a cup of water in the workspace so the residents can rinse their brushes as needed.

When the painting begins allow complete creative expression. If you notice that some residents have difficulty getting started, it may be that they need "something" to paint. Look around for themes. If it's springtime, paint pictures of flowers. If you have a resident pet, paint a picture of the pet! Let your residents follow their imaginations.

Paint Recipes...

You may want to try some of the following recipes for home-made paint.

Finger Paint

This recipe is nontoxic and edible.

2 cups flour
2 teaspoons salt
3 cups cold water

2 cups hot water
food coloring
¼ teaspoon oil of cloves
    (preservative)

Combine flour, salt and cold water. Beat mixture until smooth. Add hot water and boil until mixture becomes clear. Beat until smooth. Stir in food coloring. The clove oil is not necessary if you are using the paint within a day.

Finger Paint with Ivory Soap Flakes

¼ cup cornstarch
1 cup cold water
1 cup Ivory soap flakes
½ cup salt (preservative)

3½ cups warm water
1 cup talcum powder
1 teaspoon glycerin (optional)
food coloring or dry tempera

Mix cornstarch and cold water. Add soap flakes and salt; stir. Add warm water. Pour in a saucepan and bring to a boil, stirring constantly. Remove from heat. Beat until smooth. Add talcum powder and glycerin; mix until smooth. Add a few drops of food coloring or dry tempera for color.

Puff Paint and Sparkle Paint

These 3-D paints are easy to make. Use the following measurements for each different color.

2 tablespoons flour	food coloring or dry tempera
2 tablespoons salt	paint
2 tablespoons water	glitter (optional)

Mix the flour, salt and water in a bowl. Add several drops of food coloring (or some dry tempera paint) and stir until you get the desired shade. Pour the puff paint into plastic squeeze bottles (empty ketchup or mustard containers, for example). Now it's ready to squirt onto heavy paper, poster board, or wood. As the paint dries, it will become puffy and textured.

The salt in this recipe causes a slight sparkle when the puff paint dries. If you would like more sparkle, add a small amount of glitter to the mixture.

Watercolors

Watercolors can be made by adding food coloring to water until you to reach the desired color. The more water you use, the lighter the color will be. For vivid colors, use very little water.

...and Expressions

Fingertip Designs

Almost everyone has finger-painted at one time or another. We usually associate finger-painting with children, but many great artists such as Vincent van Gogh and Paul Gauguin have used this method.

Materials Needed: Finger paints; bowl of water; sponge; finger-paint paper; disposable latex gloves (optional).

Instruct the residents to squeeze out the sponge and run it across the finger-paint paper to slightly dampen it before painting. Residents can then scoop the paint out onto the paper. The resident can use his or her entire hand, fist, knuckles, or just one finger to spread the paint on the paper. Many different designs and patterns can be made. Movement is the benefit of this activity. Encourage the residents to tap, swirl, and wiggle their fingers across the paper.

If a resident is hesitant about putting their fingers in the paint, try using wax paper as mentioned in Blob Painting (see page 26) or keep some disposable latex gloves (like the ones that doctors use) available for the resident to use during this activity.

Variation: Monoprints. After a resident has finished finger-painting and the paint is still wet, cover the painting with another sheet of paper. Press one hand onto the paper to hold it in place, and rub the entire cover sheet with the palm of the other hand. Peel back the paper to reveal a mirror print of the painting.

Pudding Painting

This is an edible art (and a slight variation of Fingertip Designs). It is great to do with residents who may put things in their mouths. There's nothing to save from this activity— it's the process!

Materials Needed: Several colors of flavored pudding (such as vanilla, pistachio, banana and chocolate); a vinyl tablecloth or shower curtain to cover the table; damp towels to wash hands when done.

Put several piles of pudding on the table. Direct the residents by using your fingers to "paint" with the pudding on the tablecloth. Make designs with the pudding.

Coffee Can Painting

Caution: *If any of the residents in your group has a tendency to put things in his or her mouth, be advised to keep close track of the marbles during this activity.*

Prepare Ahead: If you're using liquid tempera paint, mix one teaspoon of liquid tempera in ½ teaspoon water for the consistency needed for this activity.

If using dry tempera, use ¼ cup powder to ½ cup water. The paint cannot be too thin, but it can be too thick for this activity.

Materials Needed: A one-pound or three-pound coffee can with lid for each resident; white paper cut to line the inside of each can; various colors of thinned tempera paint (prepared as mentioned above); one or two marbles per can.

Place the piece of paper inside the coffee can. Let the resident spoon or squeeze a small amount of liquid tempera paint into the can. The resident can use one or several colors. Place the marble(s) in the can and secure the lid. Let the resident shake or roll the can for a few minutes.

Coffee Can Painting can be done in pairs or groups if there aren't enough coffee cans to go around, the residents can sit around a table and roll the can back and forth to each other.

This activity can also be used to spice up an exercise program. The residents can shake the can or move it up and down or back and forth to music.

At the end of the session open up the can to see each resident's unique art creation.

Golf Ball Painting

Caution: *If any of the residents in your group has a tendency to put things in his or her mouth, be advised to keep close track of the golf balls/marbles during this activity.*

Materials Needed: A box with a lid; paper; thinned tempera paint (see Coffee Can Painting for ratios); golf balls or marbles.

This activity is similar to the marble painting. Instead of using a can, use a box with a lid. A shirt box works well or a decorated cake box from a bakery. When using a shirt box the design is a surprise when finished, but the see-through cake boxes are fun because the residents can watch their creations take place.

Place the paper in the bottom of the box, drop in the tempera paint and the golf balls (marbles can also be used for this activity). Let the resident slide the box back and forth across the tabletop in different directions. Take the lid off to see the colorful art.

Ice Cube Painting

Prepare Ahead: You will need ice cube trays, food coloring, and craft sticks, tongue depressors or Popsicle sticks. Fill an ice cube tray with water. Dye each tray (or cube area) with different colors of food coloring. Use more food coloring for darker, vivid colors and less food coloring for pastels.

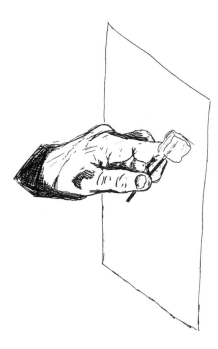

Before freezing the dyed water, place a craft stick or tongue depressor in each section of the tray. The stick will act as a handle when the water is frozen. Freeze overnight.

It generally takes four to eight hours for these to freeze depending on the freezer and the size of the cubes, so making them at least a day ahead of time is best. If you have a freezer to store them in at the facility, these "paint cubes" keep indefinitely so you can keep them in stock.

For added fun, find ice cube trays that make different shapes of ice cubes.

Materials Needed: Prepared ice cubes; white paper (finger-paint paper works very well with this activity); cloth and tape (optional).

When the colored ice is ready, show the residents how to hold the handle and rub the ice cube across the paper. They will be pleased to see the beautiful colors as the ice melts on the sheet of paper.

For residents who may not be able to hold a craft stick or even a tongue depressor, you can wrap the handle with cloth and tape to make it larger and easier to hold.

Variation: Tempera Cubes. As a variation to the water-color look, you can make frozen cubes with diluted tempera paint also.

Painting with Ice

This is just a little different from the Ice Cube Painting.

Materials Needed: Salt shakers filled with different colors of powdered tempera paint; finger-paint paper; a small ice bucket containing ice cubes; small freezer-weight plastic bags or disposable gloves.

Have the residents sprinkle several colors of tempera paint onto the white paper. They can then slip their hand in a plastic bag (or put on a pair of disposable gloves) and pick up an ice cube. Have them slide their ice cube across the paper dusted with the dry tempera powder and watch what happens!

Mirror Art

Materials Needed: Water-base felt-tip markers; a spray bottle filled with water; a mirror mounted on the wall in a convenient location or a smaller mirror to put on the tabletop; towels.

Give your residents an opportunity to create a picture on the mirror using the water-base markers. When the residents are finished, cleaning up can be just as fun. Let them squirt water on the mirror, watch the colors run, and then wipe them off with a towel.

Stained Glass Window

How about painting windows or sliding glass doors? This can be a good way to decorate for a holiday.

Prepare Ahead: Mix one tablespoon of clear dishwashing liquid with ½ tablespoon liquid tempera paint. Make several colors and put the paint in a muffin tin. This should be done right before the activity.

Materials Needed: A window to decorate; tempera paint; clear dishwashing liquid; muffin tins; paintbrushes or sponges; a damp cloth or paper towel.

Give the residents brushes or sponges and let them paint the windows. Designs may be traced onto the windows with water-base markers before painting begins if the residents desire, but encourage them to be creative.

To remove the paint from windows just use a damp cloth or paper towel.

Painting with Straws

Prepare Ahead: For this activity, use one tablespoon dry tempera to one tablespoon water, or one tablespoon of liquid tempera with ½ to one teaspoon water.

Materials Needed: Straws; various colors of liquid tempera paint; paper; shallow boxes (such as a shirt box); spoons.

Place a piece of paper in the bottom of a shirt box. Show the residents how to spoon several colors of paint onto the paper. Have them blow through their straw so that the paint blows around the paper. Be careful they don't let the end of the straw dip into the paint, or inhale the paint with the straw. Have them rotate the box so they are blowing in different directions. The designs can be beautiful. Try framing them! White tempera blown one direction on black paper gives the effect of birch trees growing.

Painting with Feathers

Materials Needed: Thin tempera in shallow bowls or pie tins; paper; turkey feathers (these can be purchased at craft stores).

This can be a fun Thanksgiving activity to encourage reminiscence. Have the residents dip their feathers into the paint and create.

Variation: Evergreen Sprigs. You can do the same thing with evergreen sprigs at Christmas time and Christmas colors of tempera paint.

Variation: Feather Dusters. To try something just a little bit different on a larger surface of paper, have the residents paint with feather dusters. A feather duster can be placed in each color of tempera paint.

Painting with Magnets

Prepare Ahead: The best tempera paint consistency for this activity is one tablespoon of dry tempera to one teaspoon water. If the paint is too thick, the paper clips won't pull through the paint; if it is too thin the idea is lost.

Materials Needed: A shirt box; a small magnet glued to the end of a ruler or stick; paper clips; several colors of liquid tempera (see above consistency ratio); paper to fit in shirt box; spoons.

Tip: Stronger magnets work best.

Have residents spoon several colors of tempera onto the paper in the box. Drop a few paper clips into the paint. Have the resident slide the magnet around under the box. Great fun and great designs!

Sponge Art

Materials Needed: Liquid tempera paint; sponges; paper; shallow dishes or pie tins.

Pour tempera into shallow dishes. Show the residents how to dip the sponge in the paint and blot it onto the paper. Anything goes here. Use many vivid colors.

This is a great activity to create wrapping paper by using large sheets of paper, or make greeting cards by using blank note cards or Manila paper cut to size. You can use this technique to decorate many different items: put a terra-cotta pot in front of your residents and let them sponge paint beautiful spring planters; decorate garbage cans; create matting for framing pictures—the possibilities are endless.

Fabric Art

Materials Needed: White T-shirts, canvas bags, aprons or nonfitted bedsheets; fabric paint; sponges; shallow dishes or pie tins.

Tip: Use fabric paint that has been slightly watered down. Check your local craft store for festive-shaped sponges to add a seasonal flare (these are inexpensive), or make your own with scissors ahead of time.

Residents can dip sponges in the paint and then decorate T-shirts, canvas bags or aprons by blotting the sponges onto the fabric. These might even sell well at a craft sale.

Variation: Creative Tablecloths. A fun idea for any holiday is to buy enough nonfitted bed sheets to cover each table in the facility dining room. Spread the sheets over a table and let the residents gather around with their festive sponge shapes (for example, hearts with pink and red paint, shamrocks with green paint, leaf-shaped sponges with paint in fall colors). When the residents are finished you will have some beautiful, reusable tablecloths for the holiday seasons.

Squeeze Painting

Materials Needed: A small sponge for each color; water dyed with food coloring; a pie tin or container for each color; large sheets of white paper or butcher paper.

Residents dip a sponge into the colored water, and squeeze out most, but not all, of the water over the paper. As each resident squeezes the excess dyed water out over their paper he or she creates a unique design with the drops and splashes of water.

Rag Painting

Materials Needed: Cotton rags cut into three-inch squares; watercolors; containers; white paper; black tempera paint and paintbrushes, or markers (optional).

Fold each piece of cloth into a small pad to use as a painting tool. Use each cloth in only one color to avoid mixing the colors together. Using either watered-down watercolors or food coloring mixed with water, dip a cloth into the paint and brush it over the paper. Show the residents how to spread large washes of color across the paper.

If they want to do a scene, show them how the colors can be the sky, ocean, or rolling hills. With a fine paintbrush and black tempera paint, they can paint in trees, boats, birds, or other details. A black marker can also be used to draw in details once the paint is dry.

Paper Towel Art

Materials Needed: Small jars of water; food coloring; eyedroppers; white paper towels or coffee filters; old newspaper.

Put a different color of food coloring in each jar of water. Place an eyedropper in each jar. Give each resident a paper towel and three to four sheets of old newspaper on which to place the paper towel. Let the residents use the eyedroppers to drip the colors onto their paper towels. As the color spots bleed and overlap, the residents will be able to see new colors forming. This can also be done with coffee filters instead of the paper towels.

Watercolors and Rubber Cement

Materials Needed: Rubber cement; a paper cup; white paper; watercolors; a tongue depressor or Popsicle stick.

Pour some rubber cement into a paper cup, then have the residents dip a stick into the paper cup containing rubber cement. The residents can wave the stick over their paper, raising it and lowering it to make a pattern of thick and thin rubber-cement lines. Put the papers aside for about fifteen minutes so the rubber cement can dry. Once dry, have the residents paint over the rubber cement pattern with watercolors. Then when the paint has dried they can rub their hand over the picture to feel the different textures.

Glue Resist

Materials Needed: White glue in squeeze bottles; heavy paper or poster board; liquid tempera; paintbrushes.

Let the residents squeeze glue designs over the paper. Let the glue dry overnight. Next let the residents brush thinned down tempera paint over the glue design. The glue will resist the paint and make an interesting work of art.

This idea can also be used to make interesting greeting cards for the residents to send for holidays or birthdays.

Soap Block Painting

Caution: *Since a potato peeler is used during this activity, you will need to determine if each resident can participate safely.*

Materials Needed: One bar of glycerin soap for each resident (Neutrogena works well because it is soft enough to carve but will not crumble away); potato peelers (if necessary, build the handle up with masking tape to make it easier for some residents to use); tempera or nontoxic acrylic paint; paintbrushes; paper.

Residents can carve designs in the soap using a potato peeler. Encourage them to dig deep into the soap. After they have completed their carving they can brush a thin coat of paint over the surface of the soap and then press a piece of paper *over* the design. Pull the paper off and there will be a print of their carved design.

Painting with Bubbles

Prepare Ahead: Either use commercial bubble solution or make your own by mixing one cup dishwashing liquid and ½ cup water. Then add one teaspoon dry tempera paint (any color) to 1 ½ cups bubble solution. Cut bottoms out of Styrofoam cups. Cover the work area with newspaper or plastic.

Materials Needed: Dishwashing liquid and water (or commercial bubble solution); dry tempera paint; Styrofoam cups; aluminum pie tins or shallow dishes (to hold paint); newspaper or plastic; Manila paper.

Show the resident how to dip the smaller end of the cup into the soap solution, and blow bubbles from the other end. Holding the cup three to four inches from the paper, have the resident blow bubbles onto the paper from the other end of the cup. The colorful designs will dry on the paper.

Vegetable and Fruit Printmaking

Materials Needed: A variety of fruits and vegetables such as oranges, apples and lettuce cut in cross sections; paper or a light-colored cotton fabric such as muslin; thick liquid tempera paint in pie tins.

Dip the vegetable sections into thick tempera paint and make prints on the paper or material. The texture of the vegetable creates an interesting effect. Broccoli and parsley are particularly fun to try. Cap mushrooms can be sliced in half and dipped in paint to make mushroom prints. This activity is extremely stimulating to the different senses.

A great vegetable to use is corn-on-the-cob. In fact, this can turn into two activities. Start with a corn shucking activity by having all the residents pulling the husk and silk off the corn. It's a wonderful reminiscing time, and the smell of fresh corn is yummy. The second half the activity is rolling the corn-on-the-cob through tempera paint and then rolling it across the paper. You may want to get corn holders for the ends of the corn to make the cobs easier to hold and roll across the paper.

Roll-On Painting

This is a favorite for some residents because it is easier for them to grip and it is not so messy, yet the process is great fun!

Prepare Ahead: Collect empty roll-on bottles. Pry off the lid with the ball and wash thoroughly. Fill bottles with liquid tempera paint and pop the ball-lid back into place. Label the bottles with the color they contain unless you can see through them.

Liquid shoe polish bottles work well for this activity, also.

Materials Needed: Roll-on containers filled with tempera paint; slick paper works best with this method.

Show the residents how to roll on their paint to create a colorful work of art. For residents who have difficulty with their fine motor skills this is a method of painting that allows them to control the outcome of their creation better than others.

Juice Painting

Materials Needed: Blueberries, raspberries, cooked beets or other colorful, juicy produce; wooden spoons; plastic bowls or containers; vinegar; paintbrushes; white paper.

For a fruit juice refresher (optional): A blender; water; berries; sugar (as needed) and cups for serving.

Have the residents crush each item of produce in a separate container with a wooden spoon. This part of the activity alone is fun and stimulates the senses as well. Let the residents taste and smell the different fruits and vegetables.

Now add a few drops of vinegar to the juices to preserve the colors when the juice is used as "paint." Now the residents are ready to paint with the fruit juice on the paper.

To make this activity a little more stimulating, save some berries to put in a blender and let the residents make some fruit juice to drink.

Watercolor Fun

Materials Needed: Paper; tape; a container of water; paintbrushes; watercolors; rubbing alcohol; eyedropper; table salt.

Tape all the edges of the paper to the table. Brush water on the paper and make sure it's completely covered. Let residents paint with watercolors—any design—onto the paper. Next let the residents drip rubbing alcohol onto the paper with an eyedropper and then sprinkle the artwork with salt. When the paint is completely dry, brush off the excess salt with a dry paper towel or your hands, and discover the results! The alcohol creates some rings in the paint and the salt make it sparkle.

Rubber Band Printing Blocks

Materials Needed: Blocks of wood; assorted rubber bands; powdered tempera; liquid starch; shallow containers; paper towels; paper.

Have the residents wrap rubber bands around the wooden blocks in any arrangement. The stretching of the rubber bands will give them a side benefit of exercising their fingers.

When the printing blocks are about ready, stir one tablespoon of powdered tempera into ½ cup liquid starch until it reaches a thick consistency. Only stir the mixture for about two minutes; the more it is stirred, the thicker it becomes. Place a paper towel in the bottom of a shallow bowl. Pour a small amount of the starch mixture onto the paper towel and spread it around with a spoon.

Instruct the residents to dip the block into the paint and then press the block onto their paper to make designs.

Tin Can Painting

This activity takes two sessions due to the drying time needed for the glue.

Materials Needed: Tin cans; a can opener; yarn or heavy string; white glue in a bowl; tempera paints; paper; meat tray or pie tin.

Remove both ends of the can. Pour some glue in a bowl. Cut a length of yarn about 10–12 inches long. Show the residents how to dip the yarn in the glue and then wrap it around the can to create a pattern or design. Add more lengths of yarn if needed. When the resident is done wrapping the string around the can, set it aside and let it dry overnight.

Once the yarn has dried on the can, pour some paint in a meat tray or pie tin. Have the residents roll their cans in the paint and then roll it over their paper to show each unique print. You may want to have a different can for each color of paint to make colorful designs.

Blob Painting

Materials Needed: White paper; several colors of thick liquid tempera; wax paper.

Have each resident drop colors of tempera onto their paper in blobs. Cover with a sheet of wax paper and let the residents use their hands to smooth the paper so the paint spreads out. The wax paper allows the resident to see the changes in the designs and colors. This also offers opportunity for movement of the arms, hands and fingers.

Let the artwork dry overnight and then peel off the wax paper. Try framing this work of art with matting and hang it in the halls. It's beautiful!

Variation: Blob Painting Surprise. This activity is similar to the activity above. Before dropping the blobs of paint on the paper, fold the paper in half. Open up the paper and let the residents drop the paint onto one side of the paper or in the fold. Then have them refold the paper and smooth over it with their hands. Open up the paper to reveal a beautiful design! They can look at their artwork when it's finished and use their imaginations to give it a name or description.

Painting the Walls

Did you know that the first paintings were painted directly on walls? Some were painted on ceilings as well. Well, let your residents try painting on the walls!

Be sure to get prior approval from administration with this activity. You may also want to do this on an outside wall.

Materials Needed: Rolls of butcher paper; paintbrushes; liquid tempera or watercolors; music (optional).

Cover a large section of a wall with butcher paper (or cover a tabletop and stand it up against a wall). Give each resident a paintbrush and some paint and let them go at it. Some may just make large strokes, while others actually paint a picture. Put some music on for added stimulation.

This can be great exercise! Have the residents stretch their arms from side to side, reaching to the right and to the left to paint. They can reach up high to paint, bend over to paint down low, or paint in circular motions. Their arms and hands can move slowly or quickly to the various tempos of the music.

Balloon Painting

This can be extremely messy so make sure you have the right place to do it, but it can be such fun and really does create beautiful art.

Prepare Ahead: Put a small amount of thinned liquid tempera inside each balloon. This is easily done by using an empty mustard squeeze container filled with the tempera.

Insert the nozzle of the squeeze bottle into the balloon fill it with a small amount of paint (about one cup for the nine-inch balloons or fill the water balloons), then blow up the balloon.

Materials Needed: Nine-inch balloons or small water balloons; watered-down liquid tempera paint; outdoor space; large sheets of butcher paper; a large metal garbage can (see variation).

Lay large sheets of paper out on the patio, sidewalk or parking lot (make sure you're clear of any cars). Residents should stand back and toss the balloons onto the paper. (Yes, the balloons will splat.) With each balloon the creation will grow.

Variation: Garbage Can Balloon Painting. If you don't have an appropriate outdoor place you can modify this activity slightly. Get a large metal garbage can. Cut a circle out of butcher paper to fit into the bottom of the can. Residents can drop or throw balloons into the can to make their designs.

Gadget Painting

Materials Needed: Paper; liquid tempera; shallow pan or dish for the paint; gadgets (such as potato mashers, empty spools of thread, rubber spatulas, lightweight rolling pins, plastic medicine cups, wrenches, or anything else you can find!)

Have the residents dip the gadgets in the paint and use them to make prints on their paper. Watch for some interesting designs.

Painting with Toothbrushes

Materials Needed: Paper; liquid tempera paint; shallow pan or dish for each color of paint; toothbrushes of various sizes.

Put out some tempera paint, paper, and the toothbrushes. This is just a different way to create with paint.

String Painting

Materials Needed: Paper; liquid tempera paint; 12-inch pieces of yarn or string.

Have the residents fold their pieces of paper in half and then unfold them. Dip the string or yarn in the paint. Place the string on the paper and refold it so a bit of the string hangs out from between the paper. Have the residents place a hand on the paper and gently pull the string out with the other. They can repeat this with several colors.

Rock Painting

Prepare Ahead: Use liquid tempera paint or mix one cup dry tempera with ¼ cup water.

Materials Needed: Collection of assorted rocks; felt-tip markers (for light-colored rocks) or tempera paint (for darker ones); paint-brushes; aerosol hair spray.

Cover the table with newspaper and place the rocks on the table. Let each resident select a rock and paint or draw designs on it. Set the rocks aside to dry. The facilitator can spray the rocks with hair spray so the color will not rub off.

Color Combinations

For an activity with paint that is less messy, try this one. It may be something to try with residents of all ability levels.

Materials Needed: Resealable plastic freezer bags; liquid starch; dry tempera.

Place two tablespoons of liquid starch in each bag. Let each resident choose two colors of dry tempera to add to the bag. Carefully zip the bag shut. Show the residents how to use their fingers on the outside of the bag to mix the paint and create new colors.

If you are working with a resident that gets into things or puts things in his or her mouth, this activity can be modified by using only edible items such as ketchup and mustard, different flavors of pudding, or flavored yogurts instead of liquid starch and tempera.

Corrugated Paper Painting

Prepare Ahead: For this activity, mix one tablespoon of liquid tempera with ½ to one teaspoon water, or one tablespoon dry tempera to one teaspoon water.

Materials Needed: Corrugated paper or cardboard; tempera paint; containers; paintbrushes.

Residents will enjoy painting on corrugated paper and watching the paint mix in the grooves to make new colors. Just give them a paintbrush, maybe put on some music and let them paint!

Texture Painting

Prepare Ahead: Mix textured substances with the tempera paint for different effects, adding one tablespoon of white glue to ½ cup tempera paint to ensure the "textures" will stick to the paper.

Some suggestions for texture substances are salt, sand, coffee grounds, cornmeal, rock salt, pine needles, or crushed peppermint candy. Some will smell pretty good also.

Materials Needed: "Textures" (such as salt, coffee grounds, cornmeal, coarse salt, pine needles, crushed peppermint candies); white glue; paper; tempera paint; paintbrushes.

Have the residents paint with these mixtures. After their paintings dry let the residents feel the different textures on the paper.

Spray Bottle Painting

Materials Needed: Dry tempera paint salt shakers; paper; spray bottle filled with water.

   If salt shakers aren't available, make shakers by poking holes in the lids of small jars (such as baby food jars).

Have residents sprinkle tempera powder on their paper. Using a spray bottle they can then spray water over the paper and the tempera powder. It's fun to watch the colors run together.

Rainy Day Raindrop Painting

There's a sense of anticipation when doing this activity.

Materials Needed: A picnic table or table that can be moved outdoors; butcher paper; stones, paperweights or tape; several colors of powdered tempera in shaker dispensers; a weather forecast for light rain!

In the morning have your residents listen for the weather forecast. If the forecast is for light rain, prepare for raindrop painting. The residents will need a table set up outside before the rain begins. Spread out the butcher paper on the tabletop and weigh it down with stones so it won't blow away.

   Have the residents sprinkle the powdered tempera randomly over the butcher paper just as the rain is beginning. Then the group can go for cover! As the rain falls onto the paper, the powdered tempera colors will blend together. When the rain stops, go out and discover what designs the rain has made for you!

   Since weather forecasts don't always cooperate, you may want to have an umbrella available in case the rain doesn't stop. Water sprinklers can also be substituted for real rain.

Sparkle Paint Art

Great for making Christmas ornaments the creative way!

Prepare Ahead: Make Sparkle Paint (see page 11 for recipe). Add a different color of tempera paint to each bottle and shake it well. You may wish to use glitter of a similar color to the paint in each bottle. Glitter will emphasize the sparkle.

Cut pieces of white poster board into festive shapes such as bells, candy canes, or stars; prepunch holes for hanging.

Materials Needed: Sparkle paint; glitter; squeeze bottles; white poster board cut into festive shapes.

Give each resident a precut shape and have them squeeze the sparkle paint onto the poster board designs. Set aside to dry for several hours. When the ornaments are dry, the salt in the paint mixture will make the ornaments sparkle.

Easel Painting

Easel painting allows an individual to express their creativity in so many ways. There is no correct or incorrect way to do this activity. There is something exciting about having a big blank sheet of paper, some paint and some paintbrushes. What opportunity! Easels can be purchased or easily made by volunteers (or yourself) ahead of time. Easels are wonderful for residents who use wheelchairs. An easel is especially welcome by residents who use wheelchairs when their wheelchair doesn't fit the height of the table. Easels can be used for painting, drawing or even writing. If you don't have any easels and can't get any right now, don't let that stop you. Follow these simple instructions for making tabletop easels.

Tabletop Easel

You can either make these yourself of have some of the more capable residents help you.

Materials Needed: A 24x36-inch piece of poster board; a straight edge or ruler; a pencil; scissors; spring clothespins to hold artwork on backing.

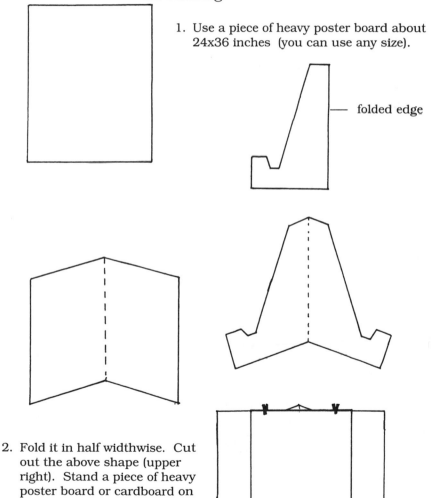

1. Use a piece of heavy poster board about 24x36 inches (you can use any size).

folded edge

2. Fold it in half widthwise. Cut out the above shape (upper right). Stand a piece of heavy poster board or cardboard on the easel and attach paper with two clothespins. Ready to paint!

Easel Paint To Music

Materials Needed: Musical recordings; a sound system; easels; spring clothespins (if using a tabletop easels); paper; paint; containers to hold paint; paintbrushes.

Put on some music while the residents are easel painting. Encourage them to listen to the music and paint to what they are listening to. Ask them what color the music sounds like to them. Classical music such as Beethoven's symphonies, Vivaldi's *Four Seasons* or other works the residents may be familiar with like "The Typewriter" and movie soundtracks work well for this activity.

Scented Easel Painting

This is a wonderful "sensory stimulation" activity. You can do this with just one scent at a time, or use several (one scent for each color).

Materials Needed: "Scents" (such as cinnamon, nutmeg or other aromatic spices, and vanilla, almond, peppermint or other extracts); easels; paper; tempera paint; paint-brushes.

Mix ground cinnamon, vanilla, peppermint or other extract into different colors of paint. The residents will want to keep painting just for the wonderful aromas!

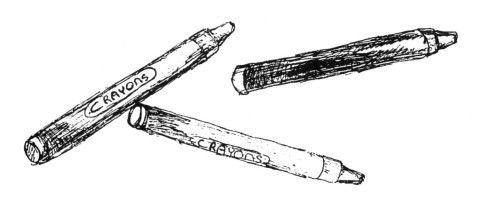

Chapter 4

Crayon Expressions

Crayons have been around for almost one hundred years, and they are often thought of only when we think about the art of young children. What are crayons? Nothing more than pigment suspended in wax! The use of pigment in wax for art actually dates back thousands of years, and has been used by many great artists such as Paul Klee, Pablo Picasso, and Hilaire Germain Edgar Degas. Just for children? Certainly not! There are many creative expressions with crayon!

Crayons can be purchased in many sizes now. You may want to invest in all sizes to accommodate the different drawing abilities of the residents. Crayola makes the most affordable, vivid colors. To eliminate the frequent interruption of peeling the paper off the crayons as they are used for drawing, soak them in a bucket of cool water overnight and then squeeze off the paper.

To make larger, easy-to-handle crayons try melting crayons in disposable muffin tins, and then let them cool. Pop the new "muffin" crayon out of the tin. Many residents will find these easier to grasp.

When heating crayons for melting, it is safest to use a double boiler instead of melting them on direct heat. Paraffin wax (the main ingredient in crayons) can catch fire over direct heat. If you don't have a double boiler you can set the crayons in disposable muffin tins and place the tin in an electric skillet filled with water set on medium (300°F).

Crayon Resist

Materials Needed: Wax crayons; water-based ink; tempera paint; watercolor paint; sponges; paintbrushes or rags.

Wax will resist water-base mediums. Your residents may want to use white crayon on white paper to make a design. They can then use a sponge or brush paint over the wax design and see what happens. Your residents may want to draw a landscape with mountains, rivers or trees with the crayon, and then paint the sky or water with watercolors.

Variation: Candle Resist. For something a little different, your residents can use candles instead of crayons.

Crayon Batik

Caution: *Only the facilitator should use the iron. Be careful—do not to burn the paper. Only use heavier grade papers for this activity, because lighter papers tear easily and scorch when ironed.*

Batik is taking the crayon-resist process one step further. You will need heavier paper such as pen-and-ink paper or medium-weight watercolor paper.

Materials Needed: Medium to heavyweight paper; wax crayons; watercolors, tempera or water-base ink; paper towels; a warm iron; an ironing board or towel.

Preheat the iron for a silk (warm) setting without steam.

Have your residents draw a thick crayon design on the paper. Next have them crumple their paper into a ball and then smooth it out again. Your residents can paint a wash of watercolors, tempera paint or ink over the crumpled picture. Next have them dab their pictures with a paper towel so the excess wash doesn't seep under the crayon. The wash will color wherever the crayon is not including the crayon flakes made while crumpling the paper.

The facilitator then irons the artwork flat by turning it over onto another sheet of paper that is placed on top of a rag. Apply the warm iron for a few seconds. Be careful not to burn the paper. Separate the sheets of paper immediately. Some of the color actually comes off onto the "cover" paper, so you have two designs if you want. If the iron is set correctly the papers won't stick together. The finished product still has a crinkly look. Just iron it flat, don't try to get all the crinkles out.

Painting with Crayons

Prepare Ahead:
Preparation time takes 15–20 minutes; give yourself a little more time if you can keep the melted wax warm so it doesn't reharden.

You will need a double boiler or disposable muffin tin and an electric skillet, and old crayon stubs of similar hues. To melt the crayons, use either a double boiler or the muffin-tin method described on page 39. With the muffin-tin method (buy the disposable aluminum ones in the grocery store) you can make several colors available. Make sure to protect the surface of the table by covering it with newspaper during this activity.

Materials Needed:
Disposable muffin tins; old crayons of similar hues (melted); cotton swabs or old paintbrushes (the brushes may not be salvageable after this activity); construction paper; newspaper to cover the table.

After the crayons have been melted, the residents can use cotton swabs or paintbrushes to dab designs onto the page. Large sweeping brush strokes don't work well with this medium, but painting with crayon makes great flowers, trees, and leaves. Have the residents watch what happens as the melted crayon cools and hardens.

Sandpaper Prints

Caution: *Only the facilitator should use the iron. Be careful not to burn the paper.*

This can be a great men's art activity, and is a great sensory stimulation activity as well.

Prepare Ahead: Cut sheets of coarse sandpaper into 5x5-inch pieces. Cut white fabric into 8x8-inch squares. Make enough for each participant.

Materials Needed: Five-by-five–inch pieces of coarse sandpaper; crayons (large crayons or muffin tin crayons work best for this activity; they are easier to handle); a warm iron; white cotton fabric (white sheets cut into eight-inch squares will work).

Preheat the iron for silk (no steam).

Have the residents make designs on the gritty side of the sandpaper with the crayons. Remind them to press down as hard as possible with the crayons. While they are doing this, discuss the texture of the sandpaper with them, and how it feels to color on the sandpaper.

When they are finished, collect the designs (one at a time) and lay the colored side of the sandpaper face down in the center of a piece of precut fabric. The facilitator will need to press the back of the sandpaper with the warm iron. When the wax melts the color is transferred from the sandpaper to the fabric.

Crayon Leaf Transfers

Caution: *Only the facilitator should use the iron. Be careful not to burn the paper.*

This is a fun autumn activity, but will definitely require careful supervision around the hot iron.

Materials Needed: Strong leaves without holes or flaws (green ones are often best); crayons; construction paper; an iron; wax paper; a thin towel (optional).

Collect strong leaves without holes or flaws. Green leaves often work best.

Preheat the iron to a medium setting (silk setting, no steam).

With bright colored crayons, residents can carefully color the back sides of the leaves (the side with the stem and veins). Each leaf may be colored all one color or several different colors. Lay a piece of construction paper on a folded towel. Have the residents arrange the leaves on top of the paper so the crayon sides are down. Cover the leaves with a piece of wax paper. (The facilitator may place a thin towel between the iron and the wax paper if they like, but it may not be necessary.) *The facilitator* will need to iron the leaves with the warm iron. Remove the leaves from the paper and leaf prints should show on the paper.

Melted Crayon Sun Catchers

Caution: Only the facilitator should use the iron.

Caution/Prepare Ahead: The facilitator or a volunteer may have to make the crayon shavings using the potato peeler, paring knife or cheese grater if it's not safe for the residents to do. Store the different colors in separate small containers.

Materials Needed: Potato peeler, paring knife or cheese grater; old crayons with the paper removed; small containers with covers; wax paper; a towel; iron.

Preheat the iron (silk setting, no steam).

Have the residents sprinkle small amounts of different colors of crayon shavings onto a sheet of wax paper. Place another sheet of wax paper over the crayon shavings. Cover the paper with a towel. The facilitator should then press down on the towel with a warm iron until the crayon shavings melt. The melted crayon design can then be cut into various shapes, such as fall leaves, butterflies or other geometric shapes, and hung in a window to catch the light.

Creating with Melted Crayons

Caution: The warming tray shouldn't be too hot, but supervise this activity carefully.

Prepare Ahead: Cover a warming tray with smooth, heavy-duty foil or two sheets of regular foil. Overlap the edges and press down so the foil doesn't slip off. Preheat the warming tray.

Materials Needed: A warming tray; unwrapped crayon stubs; pencil with an eraser; paper; an oven mitt (optional).

Once the tray is warm invite a resident to draw on the foil with the crayons. The warming tray shouldn't be too hot, but supervise this activity carefully. The crayon wax will melt on the foil. When he or she is finished, have the resident place a piece of paper over the drawing. Using the eraser end of the pencil, press the paper down carefully to remove the design. The paper should pick up the wax design from the foil. Let cool.

The foil doesn't need to be changed between residents even though a little crayon wax may be left behind. The facilitator could, however, wear an oven mitt to remove the foil if it needs to be changed. Use an oven mitt to pull off the used foil and lay a new piece of foil on the tray and when wrapping the foil around the edges to secure it to the tray.

Crayon Rubbings

Materials Needed: Paper; crayons (the "biggie" crayons work best for this activity); a variety of small, flat, textured objects such as coins, paper clips, combs, keys, sandpaper, leaves, cardboard shapes, or anything else you can think of, double-sided tape (optional).

Have residents place an item that interests them under the piece of paper, then have the residents rub with crayon over the paper until the shapes and textures appear.

This activity is easier for some residents when double-sided tape is used to position objects on the table or a cafeteria tray before placing the paper over the objects. Let the participants position their object(s) on the tape, then place the paper over top and rub.

Remember...
**It's the Process,
Not the Product.**

Chapter 5

Clay Expressions

Clay or modeling dough can be squeezed, rolled, flattened, shaped, poked, hardened, and painted. It is a wonderful therapeutic exercise for hands and fingers. As the clay warms in the resident's hand, it will become more pliable. Clay is such an expressive medium.

Clay and modeling dough can be purchased in many different colors and price ranges. Twenty-five pounds of pottery clay can be purchased for about $10. You may want to try some of the following recipes to make your own clays. Making clay is just as much fun as working with it.

Clay is a very therapeutic medium that encourages the use of fingers, hands, wrists and arms. Using any of the clay recipes or commercially bought clays like Model Magic, PlayDoh, potter's clay or modeling clay, give each of your residents a lump of clay and ask them to create something. When the residents have completed their creations, the clay can be dried and painted if desired.

Clay is an excellent medium to use when visiting a room-bound resident. As you're talking, give the resident a lump of clay. The resident may just hold it or squeeze it, but you'd be surprised at what he or she can create with it.

Clay Recipes...

Baker's Dough

4 cups flour   Food coloring
2 cups water

Mix ingredients. If mixture is too sticky, pat hands in a bowl of flour while manipulating the dough. Dough can air dry in 24 hours to save a "creation."

This clay stores well in an airtight container or resealable plastic bag. The length of time it will store depends on how often it is used.

Play Dough

1 cup salt   2 tablespoons vegetable oil
2 cups flour   2 cups water
1 tablespoon cream of tartar   Food coloring (optional)

Mix ingredients and cook over medium heat in an electric skillet or on a stove stirring constantly. Cook until the mixture forms a ball. Remove from the skillet and knead.

This clay stores well in an airtight container or resealable plastic bag. The length of time it will store depends on how often it is used.

Clay

4 cups baking soda   2 ½ cups water
2 cups cornstarch   Food coloring (optional)

Mix baking soda and cornstarch in a large pan. Add water slowly to prevent lumping. Stir well. Cook over low heat for six minutes or until the mixture has the consistency of mashed potatoes. Spread on a cookie sheet to cool and cover with a damp towel. Knead for ten minutes. If desired, add food coloring. Can be stored in an airtight container.

Cornstarch Modeling Mixture

1 cup salt   ½ cup boiling water
½ cup cornstarch   Food coloring (optional)

Combine salt, cornstarch and boiling water in a saucepan.
Cook over low heat stirring constantly until mixture is too
stiff to stir. Remove from heat and set aside. When the mixture is cool, knead until smooth.

Flavor Clay Surprise

Prepare one of the previous dough recipes without any coloring. Take some unsweetened or sugar-free Kool-Aid powder
and pour a small amount in to a hole poked in the dough.
Close the dough and give it to a resident to work with. Some
of the dough will not only start changing color, but it will
smell great as well. If you don't have any Kool-Aid, a few
drops of food coloring and a drop of an extract (such as
vanilla, orange, almond) will work.

Bread Clay

Dry, stale white bread
White glue (about 1 tablespoon per slice of bread)
A few drops of glycerin
A few drops food coloring or about 1 teaspoon tempera
     paint (optional)

Have residents remove the crust from the bread and break
the crustless bread into small pieces. They can then add
the desired amount of glue and stir it until it is mixed. Food
coloring or tempera paint can also be added to color the
dough at this time. Instruct the residents to knead the
dough with their fingers until it is pliable.

   This dough can be used to make small cookie cutter-sized
shapes and ornaments. Larger ornaments tend to break
easier.

These Sawdust Clays can be sanded and painted once dry and, therefore, can be quite popular with male residents. The second recipe usually takes a little longer to harden. To harden these clays, place them in a sunny window.

If obtaining sawdust from a sawmill, lumberyard or woodshop, sift through the sawdust carefully before using it with the residents to make the clay. Many times, what these shops give away are floor sweepings which may contain candy wrappers, nails, screws and other items that may pose a hazard to the residents. On the other hand, many shops now have self-extracting collection units to collect the dust from saws, routers and other equipment. Check around.

Sawdust Clay #1

1 ½ cups dry wallpaper paste
3 cups sawdust
Water (as needed)

Mix dry wallpaper paste and sawdust together. Slowly add water as needed until mixture becomes thick and doughy. After using this clay, allow objects to harden overnight.

This is a great clay to use with your male residents. The fact that this clay can be sanded once it dries often catches the attention of the men. This clay does not store well and should be mixed the day of the activity.

Sawdust Clay #2

2 parts fine sawdust (any kind except redwood)
1 part flour
Water (as needed)

Mix two parts fine sawdust to one part flour in a bucket. Slowly add a little water and stir. Add a little water until the mixture reaches a stiff but pliable consistency. Add more flour and water if the clay is too crumbly. Knead the clay until it becomes elastic and it is easy to shape. Store in an airtight container. Can be molded as desired and then hardened in the sun for several days. This clay hardens very well. Once this clay dries, it can be sanded and decorated with paint.

...and Expressions

Rolling Clay

Materials Needed: A lump of clay; a rolling pin; cookie cutters; table.

This is very therapeutic. While sitting at a table or bedside table give each resident a lump of clay and a rolling pin. Rolling pins can be made by filling small drink bottles with sand if you can't purchase enough wooden ones. Have the residents roll out the clay with the rolling pin using forward and backward motions until the dough is flat. Provide cookie cutters for them to cut out shapes. This activity provides great wrist and arm movement.

Variation—Cookies! Use cookie dough and have the added benefit of cookie creations. The process is the same. Add a beverage to your list and have a social with the freshly baked cookies as a centerpiece after the activity.

Toaster ovens are small, portable, and may be taken from room-to-room to provide baking activities for room-bound residents. (See chapter 11 for more ideas on Cooking Expressions.)

Cinnamon Dough Shapes

Materials Needed: Applesauce; cinnamon; bowls; spoons; rolling pins; wax paper; cookie cutters; drinking straws; access to an oven (optional).

Either prepare the following dough or have the residents prepare it by mixing about 2 cups cinnamon with ¼–½ cup applesauce. Add cinnamon to the applesauce until the mixture reaches a thick, doughy consistency similar to a rolled cookie dough.

Have residents roll out their dough on wax paper and cut shapes with a cookie cutter. Use a drinking straw to poke a hole in the top of the ornament so it can be hung up once it is dry. Allow a couple of days to air dry on the wax paper, or put in an oven (if available) or toaster oven set on warm (the lowest setting) for two hours. Smells wonderful!

Marzipan Pottery

Materials Needed: Marzipan (sold in the baking section at most grocery stores); food coloring; wax paper.

Cut the marzipan into four sections, then have the residents knead about eight drops of food coloring into each section. Use different colors for each section.

The marzipan clay can then be molded into different shapes, or each different color can be rolled into "snakes." Use the "snakes" to make coil pots. Make the bottom of the pot by winding a snake into a spiral about 1½ inches wide, then layer additional snake coils to form the sides of the coil pot. The sides can be gently pinched so the coils stick together. This makes a really colorful pot and there's no need to bake it.

Free-Form Plastic Bag Sculpture

Caution: *Follow precautions on plaster of Paris bag. Have a dust mask handy for the facilitator or volunteer who is measuring the plaster. You can premeasure the plaster mix into the bags for the residents beforehand. Don't add the water until the resident is ready since plaster sets rather quickly.*

Materials Needed: A quart-size resealable plastic bag for each resident; plaster of Paris; water.

The facilitator should measure one cup of plaster of Paris and ½ cup water into a resealable plastic bag. Be sure the bag is closed tightly with as litle air as possible inside.

Give it to a resident and let the resident mix, knead, roll, punch, bend and shape the bag with the plaster in it. As he or she works with the bag, the plaster will begin to set (about 15–25 minutes). When the plaster hardens, remove the bag to reveal his or her unique free-form sculpture. These free-form plaster sculptures can be painted if desired. Not a bad exercise activity either!

Forest Fossils

Prepare Ahead: Take a nature walk with the residents to collect the blossoms, seeds, pods, bark and leaves for this activity. When you return, or at the next meeting, continue with this activity.

Materials Needed: Plaster of Paris; water; plastic-coated paper plate or Styrofoam plate; different kinds of leaves, blossoms, seeds, pods, bark.

Mix a small portion of plaster of Paris with enough water to make mixture about the consistency of cake batter (two parts plaster to one part water). Have the residents slowly pour the plaster onto a paper plate. Before the plaster hardens, the residents can press one or two items into the plaster to make an imprint. Leave the objects in the plaster until it is almost hard (about 20–30 minutes) and then remove the object to reveal the "fossil."

Molding with Potpourri

These make wonderful smelling Christmas tree ornaments or potpourri room decorations.

Materials Needed: Potpourri (make sure the potpourri does not have pieces that are too large in the bag); white glue; old bowl or small (#1) coffee can; coffee can lids; old spoons (used only for crafts).

Have the residents mix some potpourri with quite a bit of glue in a bowl or coffee can until the mixture sticks together. It is better to have too much glue than too little since the glue dries clear. The potpourri and glue mixture can then be put on the plastic lid and shaped into a ball, wreath or other desired shape. Let dry for one to two days.

These potpourri creations will be very hard when they dry. To prepare the ornament for hanging, a straw or pencil could be stuck in before the drying period to make a hole to thread a ribbon through, or you can use a hot glue gun to attach a small loop of ribbon to the ornament after it is dry.

Sculpting with Sand

Prepare Ahead: Mix two cups of sand with one cup of cornstarch then stir in one cup of cold water. Cook over medium heat until the mixture thickens. Let the mixture cool. Store for up to two days in an airtight container.

Materials Needed: Sculpting sand (see recipe above); pencils; tempera paint.

Invite the residents to shape the sand mixture into whatever shapes they choose. Since you are using sand, you might suggest fish shapes, starfish or other ocean creatures. Show the residents how to use a pencil to make details in the wet sand mixture. Allow the sculptures to dry overnight. After the sculptures dry, the residents can use tempera paint to decorate their creations if they'd like.

Leaf Prints in Clay

Materials Needed: Leaves with stems; self-hardening clay (modeling clay, PlayDoh, or homemade playdough or clay recipe work best); wax paper; rolling pins.

Have a resident roll out the clay on the wax paper and then place the vein side (bottom) of a leaf on the clay. The resident places a second sheet of wax paper on top and rolls over the paper with the rolling pin. Remove the top sheet of wax paper and then the leaf by the stem. Place the clay print in the sun to dry.

Try this with as many different kinds of leaves as you can find. Later, see if the residents can match the impression with the leaf they used.

Potter's Clay

This clay can be purchased from craft or pottery stores.

Materials Needed: Potter's clay; bowl of water; pictures of different vessels or pots (optional).

Give each resident a lump of clay and set a bowl of water in the center of the table so the residents can moisten their fingers. The clay can be molded into many designs or the residents can try making pottery.

A pinch pot is easy to make and involves very simple instructions. Have residents form the clay into a ball. Next they can push one thumb into the center of the clay, but not through it. Have them cup one hand underneath the clay and use the other to turn the clay and pinch it with their thumb and forefinger. The opening of the pot will get larger and larger until the pinch pot is formed. Provide pencils or pipe cleaners so the resident can scratch designs into the clay if they like. When the resident is done, set aside their creation to dry (about 24 hours). The residents can then paint their creations with acrylic or tempera paint if they wish.

If the residents would like some more ideas, have pictures of different shaped vessels and pots available for them to look at if they would like to try something a little bit different.

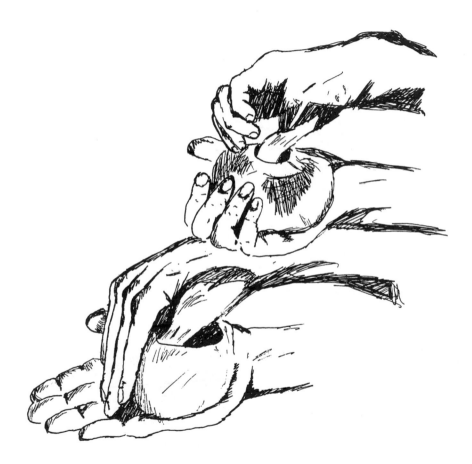

Chapter 6

Crafty Expressions

The following ideas are not too different from the ones you've read about in the previous chapters, they just don't quite fit into the paint, crayon, or clay categories. They use all sorts of items and material one wouldn't usually think of including in art activities, or take ideas one step beyond.

Let your imagination go! The ideas for creative activities are endless. Remember, the idea is to keep the residents interested and actively involved while at the same time giving them an opportunity to bring something new into existence. Remember, the idea is not to make a "craft" that looks like everyone else's. The idea is just to create. These activities can be repeated over and over and never turn out the same way twice.

Bleach Art

Caution: *Have the residents wear art smocks, aprons and/ or old clothing in case bleach splatters on them.*

Prepare Ahead: The bleach can be diluted (one part bleach to three parts water). Provide disposable gloves, and smocks or aprons for the residents.

Materials Needed: Bleach in a small container or cup; blue or black construction paper or poster board; cotton swabs and/or string; disposable latex gloves; smocks or aprons

Residents can dip the cotton swab or string in the bleach then dab it or pull it across the paper. Interesting art! Talk about what is happening to the color in the paper.

Moving Colors

This is truly fascinating and very relaxing to watch, and definitely emphasizes the importance of the process and not the product! It may even challenge the residents to discuss and discover the scientific "whys" of the activity.

Materials Needed: A pie tin; shallow tub or baking dish; 2% milk; *Sunlight* liquid dish soap. Use only these ingredients.

Pour about one inch of milk into the pan. Have the residents drop different colors of food coloring in different places in the milk. Next squeeze a few drops of the liquid dish soap into the milk. Watch what happens!

The dish soap reacts with the milk fat and causes colors to move around on their own creating a wonderful moving creation of colors. When the colors slow down, add a few more drops of dish soap and they will start up again.

Splotch Art

Materials Needed: Heavy, white drawing paper or uncoated side of poster board; dark, bright colors of tissue paper or streamers; plastic spray bottles.

First, have the residents tear the tissue paper or streamers into small scraps. This is great fine-motor exercise. Some residents may only want to do this.

Second, have the residents spray water on their paper with the water bottle. Third, have them stick the colored tissue or streamer scraps on the paper. Encourage the residents to place different colored pieces on top of each other. Fourth, instruct them to flatten the scraps on the white paper. Fifth, have them spray water over the paper and scrap collage again. Finally, they can remove all the colored scraps from the heavy paper. A colorful design will appear. Point out where the colors mixed and the new colors that were made.

Corn Syrup Creations

Materials Needed: Six-by-six–inch pieces of poster board; food coloring; light corn syrup (2–3 tablespoons per resident); cotton swabs (optional); extracts, glitter or cake decorating sprinkles (optional).

Let each resident pour the corn syrup on a piece of poster board and spread it out to the edges. Next, the resident can squeeze a few drops of food coloring of various colors on different areas of the poster board. Then encourage the resident to blend in the colors slightly with his or her fingers or a cotton swab. The process is fun, it won't hurt if the corn syrup is eaten (great for residents with Alzheimer's), and the finished product is a shiny, multicolored work of art!

For additional sensory effects, add scented extracts to the corn syrup, or sprinkle on some glitter. If you would like to keep this activity "edible" due to safety concerns, use cake decorating sprinkles instead of glitter.

Variation: Holiday Art. Let the residents paint with plain corn syrup on colored poster board cut into seasonal or holiday shapes such as red hearts, blue kites, or green Christmas trees. Small shapes can be used as Christmas decorations.

Squeezing Corn Syrup

Prepare Ahead: (This can also be done with the residents if you like.) Fill squeeze bottles with corn syrup. Add a few drops of food coloring to each bottle and shake gently. Add more coloring to make strong, bright shades if necessary.

Materials Needed: Large paper plates; light corn syrup; food coloring; squeeze bottles; music (optional).

If you choose to have the residents help you prepare the bottles of dyed corn syrup, bring some background music along and have the residents shake the bottles to the music. The facilitator should be able to help with the final shaking.

Have the residents squeeze the dyed syrup onto their paper plates in drops. Once several colors are on their plates, have the residents tip their plates back and forth so that the colors blend and create new colors. Beautiful designs will form. Set the plates aside and allow them to dry for several days.

Variation: Holiday Decorations. This activity can also be done on poster board cut into holiday shapes to make Christmas tree decorations.

Creating with Tissue Paper

Prepare Ahead: Thin one cup of white glue with three tablespoons water. This can be stored in an airtight container until needed.

Materials Needed: Several colors of tissue paper torn or cut into a variety of small shapes; white glue and water mix (prepared as mentioned above); paper; brushes.

Invite the residents to brush a piece of paper with the thinned glue. Have the residents choose pieces of colored tissue paper and place them on their paper while overlapping the different shapes and colors to create new shapes and colors. Have the residents apply a second coat of glue and allow it to dry. The colors of the tissue paper will bleed and create beautiful designs.

Buttermilk Drawings

Materials Needed: Sponges; buttermilk in a shallow pan; finger-paint paper; colored chalk (thick sidewalk chalk works well for this activity).

Have the residents sponge a thin layer of buttermilk over the finger-paint paper, then let them draw on the paper with colored chalk. This process will create thick, smooth chalk drawings.

Spaghetti Art

Prepare Ahead: Boil water to cook the spaghetti. Before placing the spaghetti noodles in the water, add a small amount of cooking oil to the water. Cook the spaghetti until it is soft, but do not overcook it. Drain. Rinse the spaghetti with cold water until it is cool enough to handle.

Materials Needed: Cooked spaghetti noodles; black construction paper; wax paper and heavy books (optional).

Place a bowl of noodles on the table and give each resident a black piece of construction paper. They are now ready to begin designing with the spaghetti. The starch in the noodles will make them stick to the paper. The residents can shape the spaghetti into flowers, faces, landscapes, or any other designs they like.

If you would like to keep these creations, cover the artwork with a piece of wax paper and put a heavy book on top of it so that it will dry flat.

Variation: Pasta Art. For a greater variety of shapes and sizes, try this activity with other pastas, such as lasagna, wagon wheel pasta or elbow macaroni.

Shredded Wheat Art (Christmas Wreaths)

Materials Needed: Large-size shredded wheat cereal biscuits; bowls or plastic containers; green food coloring; white glue; small margarine or coffee can lids; small red beads or cinnamon red hots (candy); red ribbon or yarn.

Have each resident crumble one large shredded wheat biscuit into a bowl. Stir five drops of food coloring into $\frac{1}{4}$ cup white glue and add to the cereal. Mix the green glue and shredded wheat together until the cereal is completely coated. Have the residents pile their mixture on top of a small margarine lid and shape it into a wreath, then let the residents decorate the wreaths by pressing red beads or cinnamon red hots into the green mixture. While the wreaths are still partially wet, the facilitator can make a hole at the top of the wreath with a pencil point to insert ribbon or yarn for hanging. Leave the wreath on the plastic lid to dry. The wreathes will dry in about 24 hours. Peel it off the lid. The facilitator should add the ribbon (sometimes it's easiest to use a needle to insert the yarn or ribbon) and tie it off. Now it's ready to be used as a Christmas decoration.

Although with this activity you will have a finished product, it is the finger and hand movement while crumbling the cereal and stirring the glue that is therapeutic.

Scissor Art

The most familiar scissor art is the snowflake cut out of white paper. Cut-paper designs are simple and can produce some very creative artwork.

Materials Needed: Colored paper; scissors; pencils (optional).

Show residents how to fold paper in half once or several times. The residents may cut off the corners or cut into edges with the scissors. They shouldn't cut off the edges or they might remove the fold holding the paper together.

If they would like they can draw a design to cut out of a piece of paper that is folded in half only once. This will produce a symmetrical cut paper design.

Glue Designs

Prepare Ahead: Colored glue can be purchased, but it is much more expensive and can be made so easily instead.

   To make colored glue, mix about two tablespoons of dry tempera into one cup of white glue—add more or less tempera to vary the color. (You may also use food coloring to dye white glue.) This can be mixed in the bottle by tilting and squeezing the bottle, or stirred in a bowl and poured into a squeeze bottle. Store in an airtight squeeze bottle or container until use.

Materials Needed: Poster board or cardboard; squeeze bottles; colored glue.

Residents can squeeze designs onto the poster board and make colorful, shiny creative pictures. Let the creations dry for about 24 hours. When the creations dry, they have a wonderful soft shine and texture.

Wire Sculpture

The wire for this activity can be anything from craft supply wire to solder wire as long as it is flexible enough for the residents to shape. Use copper or brass wire for color variation.

Prepare Ahead: Cut wire into two-foot lengths with wire cutters or heavy scissors.

Materials Needed: Thin wire; pencils or short pieces of dowel sticks to make coils; clay or Styrofoam bases in which to set the sculpture; spray paint (optional).

Residents can bend and coil wire to create what they would like. They may want to start by sticking one end in the base and then forming their sculpture from there. Show them how to wind thin pieces of wire around a pencil to make a spiral shape before attaching it to their sculpture. The wire can be spray painted when the sculpture is completed.

Some easy and interesting shapes to suggest are Christmas trees, flowers, sailboats and people. Remember, however, it is their creation!

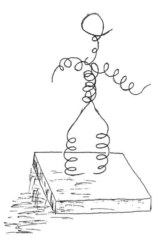

Designing with Sawdust

Here's another activity that appeals to many male residents. It must be the sawdust!

Materials Needed: Light colors of dry powdered tempera paint mixed with sawdust; shallow boxes or trays; dark-colored construction paper; white glue; squeeze bottle for glue or old paintbrushes.

The colored sawdust can either be mixed ahead of time, or can be done by a resident in a few minutes. Mix one part dry tempera to three parts sawdust.

Have the residents place a piece of construction paper in the shallow box or tray, and draw a design on the paper with the glue. The glue can be painted onto the paper with an old paintbrush, or squeezed onto the paper straight from the bottle. Then let the residents sprinkle the colored sawdust over the glue. Once the glue dries, the excess sawdust is shaken off to reveal a unique design.

The excess colored sawdust may be stored in a plastic bag for future use.

Designing with Wood Shapes

This is another good creative activity for male residents. Wood shapes and pieces can be purchased at a craft store or you can go to a lumber yard and ask for scraps.

Materials Needed: Wood shapes or scraps; pieces of poster board, cardboard or wood; white glue; sandpaper (optional).

Have the residents glue the wooden shapes onto pieces of wood, poster board or heavy cardboard. Residents may even enjoy sanding the wood before gluing it together.

Locking Blocks

Caution: Use the larger blocks when working with residents who might try to put things in their mouths.

Materials Needed: Lego-type locking blocks.

Using Lego-type blocks, you can offer your residents the opportunity to build. This also can be very popular with male residents. Although you may initially think this is a child's activity, Lego-type building blocks can be enjoyed by people of all ages. These blocks can be purchased in a variety of sizes and colors.

Foil Art

Materials Needed: Aluminum foil (supply different thicknesses if possible); white glue; construction paper.

Invite the residents to work with sheets of aluminum foil by crumpling, twisting, tearing and wadding it into different shapes. Have them glue their shapes onto the construction paper. Try using different thicknesses of aluminum foil to create different effects. Each thickness of foil feels different in the resident's hands, and behaves differently when they work with it.

Papier-Mâché Art

Papier-mâché is very inexpensive and can be used in a variety of ways. Premixed papier-mâché can be bought at craft stores (just add water), or you can make your own from flour and water (ratio of 1:1) and old newspaper. This is a messy activity so be sure to cover the tables and have the residents wear aprons or smocks.

Prepare Ahead: Inform the residents to wear aprons or smocks. Cover the tables.

Materials Needed: Papier-mâché (or flour and water to make your own); old buckets or tubs and something to stir papier-mâché; newspapers; items to mold papier-mâché around; plastic to cover table; petroleum jelly (optional).

Have residents tear two-inch wide strips of newspaper (a great activity in itself). Mix the papier-mâché in old buckets or tubs.

Many things can be used as a mold for papier-mâché— blow up balloons, use bowls, tin cans or paper towel tubes. If using a bowl or can, smear it with petroleum jelly before covering it with the papier-mâché. This will make it easier to separate the bowl from the papier-mâché when it dries.

Have residents cover the outside of the mold with paper strips dipped in the mâché mixture. Show them how to overlap the pieces so that the entire mold is completely covered with several layers of newspaper. Let dry for about 24 hours. Pop the balloon, or take the shape off the bowl or other mold. Residents can then paint and decorate their papier-mâché creation. If a balloon is used as the mold, the papier-mâché shape can then be made into a puppet or piñata for further fun!

Yarn Art

Materials Needed: Twelve-inch lengths of yarn of various colors, thicknesses and textures; liquid starch in a bowl; wax paper.

Show residents how to dip a piece of yarn into the liquid starch. Have them hold the yarn over the bowl for a short time to let the excess starch drip off. The residents can then arrange the yarn on the piece of wax paper and keep adding other pieces of yarn to create a design. Separate pieces of yarn should touch for best results with this activity.

Let the design dry overnight. When the design is completely dry, the wax paper can be peeled off leaving the yarn design.

Marshmallow Art

This activity offer the opportunity to be creative and is definitely the *process* not the product. Residents also receive some sensory stimulation benefits from touching the soft, squishy marshmallows and the rougher styrofoam. This is also a hand movement opportunity.

Materials Needed: Marshmallows (various sizes and colors); toothpicks; Styrofoam blocks.

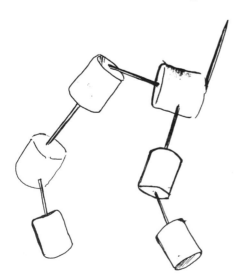

Show the residents how to begin by poking a toothpick into the styrofoam, add a marshmallow to the end of the toothpick and continue to add toothpicks and marshmallows to the sculpture.

Marshmallows of different sizes and colors can add to this activity. Large marshmallows can be used for residents having trouble with fine motor skills.

Poke Art

This is another activity where the benefit is in the process. Some of the benefits of this activity are fine motor movement, olfactory stimulation, tactile stimulation and creative fun.

Materials Needed: Toothpicks (plain or colored); short lengths of colored craft chenille stems (6–8 inches long); fruits or vegetables that can be poked by the residents (such as cucumbers, bananas, apples, oranges, lemons, grapefruit, bell peppers or other firm produce; avoid hot peppers though since the oil in hot peppers can be irritating to both the eyes and skin).

No special purpose to this one. Poking is fun, and with all the fruits and vegetables it is sure to stimulate the senses. The chenille stems can bend and be woven through other chenille stems.

Poking the toothpicks or chenille stems into the fruit and vegetables, and bending and twisting the chenille stems is great exercise. This process also releases the aroma of the fruit or vegetable. The finished product is a "crazy" creation, but the conversation that takes place while doing this activity is an added benefit. The repetitive motion of the poking makes this a good activity to try with Alzheimer's patients too. Save some fruit for a snack afterward!

Pretzel Art

Materials Needed: Pretzels; white frosting or white glue; poster board.

Pretzels come in all shapes and sizes. Place many varieties of pretzels in the center of the table and let the residents create pictures and designs with pretzels by adhering them to the poster board with glue or frosting—if they don't eat all the pretzels first!

When purchasing the pretzels don't forget the giant soft ones as well as the small skinny ones. Use the white frosting as the "glue" if you want to keep these creations completely edible.

Cracker Art

Materials Needed: Cookie sheets or heavy paper plates; assorted crackers such as Triscuit, Ritz, saltines and Goldfish; peanut butter; plastic knives or tongue depressors; assorted colorful candies such as jelly beans or M&Ms (optional).

The peanut butter is the "glue" that will hold the creation together. Show the residents how to spread the peanut butter on the top or edge of a cracker to attach it to another. They can build towers, castles, bridges or anything they choose with the crackers—if they don't eat them first!

Men seem to enjoy this activity because it involves both food and building. The candies are optional but can be used to add a little more color or decoration.

Fish Prints

Prepare Ahead: You will need to go to a fish market and buy a whole fish. Keep it frozen. Only one fish is needed if the group is small; the residents can take turns.

Materials Needed: A whole fish; washable ink (any color); newspaper; butcher paper or lightweight white paper; paintbrushes.

Lay newspaper over the table. Have a resident paint the frozen fish with ink. Show them how to lay a piece of paper over the fish and then press lightly to print the fish onto the paper. Peel away the paper and let it dry. There will be a print of a fish on the paper. There's no need to rinse off the fish between turns; pass the fish to the next resident. The process of painting the fish and pressing the paper is fun and different.

Reminiscence is an added benefit of the activity. Don't be surprised to hear the residents talking about their favorite ways to cook fish while waiting their turn, or start telling "fish" stories about the ones that got away.

Creating with Fingerprints

Prepare Ahead: Make paint pads by lining each aluminum pie pan with felt and soaking the felt with thick tempera paint (store-bought ink pads can also be used but make sure the ink is washable and non-toxic). Make a separate pan for each color of ink.

Materials Needed: Aluminum pie tins lined with felt; thick tempera paint; paper; crayons; washable markers; pens.

Show the residents how to press their fingertips against the paint-soaked pad and then onto the paper to make fingerprints and designs. The crayons, markers and pens can be used to add features to their fingerprints.

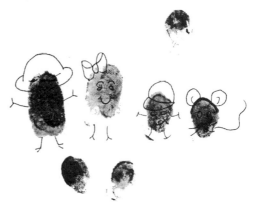

Sun Catchers

Caution: *Only the facilitator should use the toaster oven and handle the warm plastic.*

Materials Needed: Short, clear, hard plastic cups (can be found in party shops or craft stores); permanent or transparency markers; a toaster oven (or a facility oven); yarn; scissors; pencil to punch hole.

Give each resident a plastic cup and have them draw designs on the outside of cup with the markers. When the resident is done, place the cup in the toaster oven set on *low* (about 200°F). The cups can be placed either upright or upside down in the toaster oven, but it will produce a slightly different outcome. Try both! The plastic will melt into a round disk. While the plastic is still warm, punch a hole in the disk so you can insert yarn for hanging it up when the plastic is cool. Hang the disk in the window so it catches the sunlight.

Bubble Pop Art

Caution: *Warn the residents to not inhale when using the straw.*

Materials Needed: Liquid dish soap; water; food coloring; cups; straws; light-colored construction paper; markers or crayons (optional).

Mix a little dish detergent in a half-full cup of water; add food coloring and stir. Set the cup in the center of the paper. Have your residents dip the end of the straw into the cup and blow bubbles continuously so that the bubbles spill over the side of the cup and pop on the paper. *Remind the residents not to inhale.* When the bubbles pop, there will be a unique colored design left on the paper. If they choose to, the residents can trace around the design with marker or crayon.

Make sure to offer this activity to room-bound residents. This activity can be great respiratory exercise and can be beneficial to residents that spend a lot of time in bed. The deep breathing and exhaling in this activity can help bed-bound residents avoid pneumonia and other respiratory infections caused by being in bed for long periods of time.

Popcorn Art

Prepare Ahead: Make popcorn in a hot-air popper, or turn this into two different activitiesby adding a popcorn popping party. The residents can enjoy this snack but be sure you make enough popcorn for the art activity, too.

Materials Needed: Popped popcorn; powdered tempera paint (several colors); resealable plastic bags; glue; poster board or heavy paper; green yarn or chenille stems (optional).

Residents can color the popcorn by putting a powdered tempera color into a resealable plastic bag with the popcorn and shaking the bag until the popcorn is well-coated. Do this with several colors. The residents can glue the colored popcorn onto their papers to make a colorful work of art. Colored popcorn makes very pretty flowers. Just add green yarn or chenille stems for the stems.

Variation: Popcorn Garlands. Popcorn is also great for making holiday garlands. Use needles and thread to string the colored popcorn into long strands of garland.

Chenille Art

Materials Needed: Chenille stems; poster board and glue (optional).

Provide a resident several colorful chenille stems to twist and shape and even link together. This can occupy a resident for quite a long time. For a more permanent creation provide a piece of poster board for them to attach the chenille stems with glue.

Felt Art

This is a great activity to take from room to room for the room-bound residents. It can also be done as a group activity with each person adding another piece to the creation.

Prepare Ahead: Make a flannel board by covering a piece of cardboard with cotton flannel or felt material. This board can be any size. Cut the fabric slightly larger than the board, fold the fabric over the edges and secure on the back side only with hot glue or staples.

Materials Needed: A flannel board; an assortment of colored felt cut in various shapes.

The felt pieces stick to the flannel board. Give the residents and opportunity to create a design or picture with the felt.

Cotton Ball Collage

Materials Needed: Cotton balls (various sizes and colors); glue; paper or poster board; cotton batting; gauze or scraps of cotton fabric (optional).

Cotton balls can be purchased in different sizes and colors. Put a variety of cotton in the center of the table along with some glue. Residents will enjoy the soft feel of the cotton as they glue it on to paper or poster board. Use this activity as a reminiscing opportunity and talk about what cotton reminds them of, and how they used to use cotton.

If you would like to add a little variety, bring other cottons like cotton batting, gauze and scraps of cotton fabric (any color as long as it's cotton). The cotton batting and fabric scraps may even invite conversations about quilting or sewing.

Paper Clip Art

This can provide activity for residents who experience agitation or just want something to do, and it's great fine motor exercise for the fingers. Paper clips can be found in bulk at office supply stores.

Materials Needed: Colored paper clips (larger sizes).

Give the residents a pile of paper clips to link, unlink and create designs. You might even try to have a contest with the residents to see how long they can make a paper clip chain!

Creating with Shaving Cream

Caution: *If you think a resident might try to eat the shaving cream, use whipped cream instead.*

This activity can be done right on top of the table, but it is advisable to cover the table with a plastic tablecloth or shower curtain to make cleaning easier. You can also give each resident their own individual cafeteria tray to create on. This activity stimulates the senses. It smells wonderful!

Prepare Ahead: Cover the work area with a plastic table cloth or shower curtain and provide a cafeteria tray for each resident.

Materials Needed: Several cans of shaving cream (or whipped cream); plastic to cover tables; cafeteria trays (optional).

Squirt some shaving cream in front of each resident (or if they are able let them do it themselves) and let residents create and sculpt with it. Great fun!

The whipped cream works great with residents who try to eat things or put things in their mouths.

Sandpaper Webs

Materials Needed: Sheets of sandpaper; pieces of different colors of yarn about a foot long.

Show the residents how to use the yarn pieces to create webs on the sandpaper by arranging the yarn in any design they desire. The yarn will stick to the sandpaper. This is a good tactile stimulation activity and can occupy a resident creating and recreating designs. Remember, it's the process, not the product.

Yarn Art "Stained Glass"

Materials Needed: Twelve-inch to 24-inch lengths of brightly colored yarn (various colors); brightly colored tissue paper; white glue; water; bowl.

Stir two tablespoons white glue with two tablespoons water in the bowl to thin the glue.

Have residents soak the yarn in the thinned glue and then squeeze the yarn through their fingers to remove the excess. They can then press the yarn pieces to the tissue paper creating a design. Allow to dry overnight. Trim the excess tissue from the edges.

These designs can be hung in front of a window or used to create a mobile.

Creating with a Geoboard

Prepare Ahead: To make a geoboard you will need a piece of wood (about 8x11 inches), finishing nails and a hammer. Try to find nails with round heads so the residents are less likely to get scratched or cut on them. Burrs on the nails may be removed or smoothed with a metal file.

Start by mounting small finishing nails securely into the piece of wood. Place the nails in rows at equal distances about one inch apart. Leave about ¾ inch of each nail above the board.

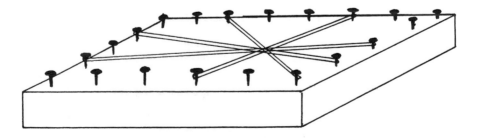

Materials Needed: A geoboard; small multicolored rubber bands; colored pencils; paper cut into the size of the geoboard with dots to represent the nails.

Provide materials. Show the residents how to create designs by stretching the rubber bands from one nail to another and then how to transfer the design to the paper. Once a resident makes a simple design on the geoboard, they can draw it on the dotted paper if they choose. Some residents may just want to create and re-create on the geoboard.

Paper Tube Sculpture

Prepare Ahead: Collect toilet paper, paper towel and wrapping paper tubes of various widths. You may want to cut these into various lengths and at different angles ahead of time depending on the abilities of the residents.

Materials Needed: Toilet paper, paper towel and wrapping paper tubes; scissors; pieces cardboard for a base; white glue; tempera paint; paintbrushes (optional).

Show the residents how to get started by gluing paper tubes onto the cardboard base and then have them keep building. If the residents can safely make intersections in the tubes, allow them; if not, make a few intersect cuts yourself. Allow the glue to dry. The sculpture can be painted once dry.

Creating with PVC Pipe

Prepare Ahead: PVC pipe can be purchased at hardware stores and home improvement centers. It comes in various lengths, widths and shapes, and makes wonderful "put togethers." Purchase several joints and reducers so the pieces can be connected.

Materials Needed: PVC pipe, joints and reducers of various lengths, widths and shapes.

Place the PVC pieces in a large basket on a table. Provide plenty of tabletop space and invite the residents to have fun creating structures.

Button Creations

Save all those old buttons! Buttons may also be purchased in bulk quantities from craft catalogs, craft stores, fabric stores and some clothing outlets.

Materials Needed: Buttons; poster board or cardboard; glue; old paintbrushes.

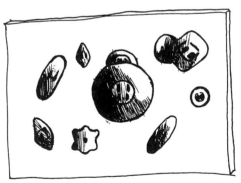

Residents can squirt or place drops of glue on their poster board in designs or they can brush the entire piece of poster board with glue. It's a little harder to handle the buttons when they have glue on them, but if the residents want to put the glue on the buttons then place the button on the poster board, it can be done that way, too. Have them create designs with the buttons!

Variation: Button Frames. Cut the poster board out into a picture frame shape and they can decorate the "frame" with buttons. The frames can then be used to mount the residents' artwork from other days.

Puzzle Creations

This is the same idea as the button creation above. Instead of using buttons, use pieces of jigsaw puzzles. Everyone has old jigsaw puzzles lying around (sometimes with a piece or two missing). If not, try garage sales.

Materials Needed: Jigsaw puzzle pieces; poster board or cardboard; glue.

The residents can glue the puzzle pieces, picture side up, on the poster board in any design they like. The pieces don't have to connect.

Variation: Jigsaw Frames. Using jigsaw puzzle pieces also makes great picture frames for the residents' artwork. See button frames for details.

Ocean Waves

You will need to make these for the residents. This bottle is great for promoting relaxation and it's interesting to watch.

Materials Needed: A one-liter, clear plastic soda bottle with cap (the smaller sizes such as 24-ounce work well also); water; vegetable oil; blue food coloring; heavy tape; sequins or glitter (optional).

First, fill half the soda bottle with water. Add vegetable oil until the bottle is three-quarters of the way full. Add a few drops of blue food coloring to the bottle. Screw the cap on tightly and secure it with heavy tape.

The first time the bottle is used, have the resident shake it up so the food coloring dyes the water. Then show the resident how to tilt the bottle back and forth slowly. The action will cause the contents of the bottle to look like ocean waves. Very soothing!

For little variety, you can use other colors of food coloring or even add sparkly sequins or glitter to the water.

Sandwich Bag Designs

Caution: *Only the facilitator should handle the iron.*

Materials Needed: Plastic sandwich bags; aluminum foil; iron; scissors; flat items to put inside the bags such as foil stars, confetti, glitter, sequins, ribbon, lace.

Preheat the iron to warm (wool setting).

Have the resident place their plastic bags on top of a piece of aluminum foil that is slightly larger than the bag. Have the residents select items to place inside their bag. Don't fill the bag too much since some space will need to be left for the plastic to stick together. Place a second piece of aluminum foil on top of the resident's plastic bag; press the foil with a warm iron. Allow to cool a few minutes, then peel away the foil. The plastic can be trimmed with scissors to make a shape once it is cool if a resident desires.

Rainbow Creations

This is another example of how several of the creative art forms can be combined.

Materials Needed: An overhead projector; transparency sheets; transparency markers or dry erase white board markers in a variety of colors; a tape or CD player; music (classical or instrumental works best); slide projector and slides (see variation).

Play music to set the mood. Place the markers in the center of the table for the residents to share and give each resident a transparency sheet. Ask the residents to think about rainbows. Perhaps you could also read a poem about rainbows to start and maybe show some pictures of rainbows. Instruct the residents to use the markers to "create" a picture on the transparency which reminds them of rainbows. Encourage them to use their imagination and not just draw an arc of colors. Have them listen to the music and think about their colors.

When everyone is finished, turn on the overhead projector so that the large light shines on a wall. Turn out the room lights, replay the music, and show the series of "rainbows" the residents have created. There should be a beautiful splash of color on the wall.

Variation: Rainbow Slides. This same idea can also be done using a slide projector and giving the residents blank slides to draw on. This may be too difficult for some residents, but the more able ones enjoy seeing their tiny creation projected and enlarged on a wall after it is done.

Computer Art

Materials Needed: A computer; drawing or painting software; a printer (if you have a color monitor, it is best to have a color printer too); computer paper.

Don't rush out and buy a computer. If you have access to one though—great! There are many basic drawing and painting programs that can give your residents an opportunity to create computer art. For many of your residents this will be their first exposure to a computer. At first they may hesitate, but soon they will become comfortable with it, and may begin to get very excited when their art is printed.

At one facility, the activity director had a Macintosh with some basic drawing and painting programs that she made available to the residents. The activity director would open the program and give the residents some simple initial instructions about how to use the mouse, and how to use some of the basic drawing tools, and the residents would start creating. Very few residents had any problems after they got over the initial intimidation of using a computer.

Collage Expressions

If the residents are unable to use scissors or tear out the shapes themselves for these activities, this would be a good preparation activity for a volunteer.

Collage of Shapes

Prepare Ahead: Cut squares, circles and triangles in different sizes from various colors and patterns of wallpaper sample books.

Residents who can use scissors safely may help with preparation. It takes a while to cut enough shapes for this activity.

Materials Needed: Prepared shapes cut from wallpaper sample books; white glue; paper or cardboard.

Let the residents create a colorful collage from the shapes and patterns of wallpaper by gluing the colorful shapes to their paper.

Carpet Collage

Prepare Ahead: Cut carpet samples into different shapes and sizes. Since this is easier to do with an Xacto knife, it is best to have a volunteer do it, or do it yourself.

Materials Needed: Carpet remnants or carpet samples cut into different shapes and sizes; cardboard or poster board; white glue.

Have the residents glue the pieces of carpet onto the cardboard. The added benefit is that this is a good tactile stimulation activity.

Coupon Collage

Something fun to do with all those Sunday coupons! A great conversation starter as well. You may get a real kick out of listening to your residents talk about grocery shopping and the change in prices.

Materials Needed: Sunday coupon sections; scissors; paper; white glue.

Have the residents choose coupons from the pile in the center of the table, clip or tear out the coupons, and incorporate them into a collage. It's fun and colorful when finished. They may even have their best time collecting the coupons!

Smile Collage

Materials Needed: Old magazines; scissors; paper; white glue.

Put on some happy or lively music and provide residents with magazines to search for people smiling. They can either clip or tear out the smiling faces to glue on the paper for a collage.

Grab Bag Collage

Prepare Ahead: Fill up several paper sacks (one for each resident) with assorted scraps of paper, yarn, sequins, tissue paper, ribbon and other small odds-and-ends. Make the grab-bag items as different as possible!

Materials Needed: A grab bag for each resident; paper; white glue.

Let each resident select a sack without seeing what's inside. Give each of them a piece of paper and some glue to create a collage with their grab bag items.

Nature Clay Collage

This is also a great nature activity. Take the residents on a nature walk to collect twigs, acorns, leaves, bark, wild flowers, rocks, pebbles, shells and other items that interest them if possible. Leaves and wild flowers can be pressed in wax paper between the pages of a heavy book overnight to preserve them if you cannot schedule the activity immediately following the nature walk, or if the residents would like to keep their collage. Self-hardening clays are best if the resident plans on keeping their creation.

Materials Needed: Clay; twigs, acorns, leaves, bark, wild flowers, rocks, pebbles, shells, or other items with a nature theme.

Give the residents a lump of clay and a selection of items from nature. Have the residents stick the different nature items into the clay to create a nature collage.

When working with Alzheimer patients remember it's the *process* that counts. The facilitator can use a clay that won't harden and remove the items after the activity when working with Alzheimer's patients. The clay and the items can then be reused.

Junk Sculpture

Materials Needed: Styrofoam blocks or packing pieces or a lump of clay; odds-and-ends such as paper clips, spools, nuts, bolts, pieces of wire or chenille stems, pencils (may be unsharpened), metal washers, bottle tops, and old utensils.

This may not be a "junk" sculpture on a grand scale, but it gives the residents, especially men, an opportunity to be creative with what they have. Show them how to stick items down into the Styrofoam and how to attach the different objects together with the wire or chenille stems. Show them how to wind thin pieces of wire around a pencil to make a spiral shape before attaching it to their junk sculpture.

Chapter 7

Nature Expressions

There is nothing quite as beautiful, stimulating, or relaxing as nature. Creating with items from nature can also offer sensory stimulation and many opportunities for therapeutic activity. Planting seeds or tending a garden offers an opportunity for creative expression, but there's so much more.

Ice Sculpture Art

Prepare Ahead: Fill a large mixing bowl with water and freeze it solid. Once frozen, remove the large piece of ice from the bowl and place it on a cafeteria tray or in a shallow pan.

Materials Needed: Ice; food coloring (various colors); a cafeteria tray or shallow pan; eyedroppers (optional).

If you have food coloring in dropper bottles, great; let the residents use those instead of the eyedroppers. If not, let the residents use eyedroppers and take turns squeezing food coloring onto the ice.

Watch how the colors run down and through the ice and how the colors mix. It's very interesting to watch and may occupy residents for a very long time.

Ice Castles

You will want the residents to bring gloves or else provide gloves for the residents during this activity. In Texas, most people don't have gloves so I keep inexpensive gardening gloves on hand for many activities instead.

Prepare Ahead: Fill block-like containers with water and freeze. This usually takes 24 hours for the larger blocks.

You can use square or rectangular plastic containers, cottage cheese containers, yogurt containers, or anything else that's a suitable size for the residents. When you are ready to unmold the frozen blocks, briefly dip the containers into warm water. Also, make a lot of ice cubes.

Materials Needed: Blocks of ice; ice cubes; gloves; a tray to work on.

Have the residents put their gloves on—now they are ready to build! Put the ice (blocks and cubes) in the center of the table on a tray and have the residents work together stacking the ice to make an ice palace. They will need to hold the pieces of ice together for a few seconds before the ice will stick in place.

Building Snowmen (or Snowwomen)

This activity does not rely on living in a cold winter climate. You can even do this in the middle of a Texas summer. I do! And you don't have to go outside.

Prepare Ahead: If you don't have access to snow, find a source of crushed or shaved ice, such as an ice machine, or make your own. Have your residents bring their gloves.

Materials Needed: Gloves; snow (or you may substitute finely crushed or shaved ice); cafeteria trays; baby carrots, raisins and twigs to decorate the snow people.

If it *is* winter, and you *do* live where there is snow on the ground then just bring some inside and pile it on cafeteria trays. If you don't have snow, then crushed or shaved ice from an ice machine will do. Have the residents wear gloves and sit around a table while they build their snowman together. Be sure to provide them with a baby carrot for a nose, raisins for eyes, and some twigs for arms!

Variation: Traditional Snowpeople. If you do live in a snowy climate and the elderly you work with are physically able to go outside, you might consider brief snowman building activities outside.

Sand Sculpture

If you've ever been to the beach you have probably done this. There won't be a lasting product from this activity, but the process is fun and offers tactile stimulation.

Materials Needed: Sand (can be purchased at a garden center, nursery, and some toy stores); water; buckets or large bowls; cafeteria trays or plastic shower curtains to cover the work area; small molds or containers (optional).

Have your residents mix the sand with water in buckets or bowls until it begins to clump and stick to itself. They can make their creations either on cafeteria trays or directly on the covered tabletop. By taking some of the wet sand in their hands they can squeeze it out onto the surface and make tall formations or smaller ones. Let the residents be creative. If the sand doesn't hold a formation, then it is too wet.

You may even want to have a sand castle contest. Give your residents sand molds, buckets or small containers to use with the damp sand on a cafeteria tray. Show them how to pack the sand into the molds and turn it over onto the tray. The sand should be damp enough to keep its form.

Creative Colored Sand

Prepare Ahead: Colored sand can be purchased, but it is less expensive to make it yourself by adding food coloring or dry tempera to the sand.

Materials Needed: Different colors of dry sand in containers; small, clear jars with lids; small scoops; funnels (optional).

The clear jars for this activity can be anything from baby food jars (these work great) to jelly-size canning jars.

Put several different colors of sand in containers on the table with a scoop in each container. Give each resident a small, clear jar. Show them how to scoop the sand into their jar to create layers. Jars should be filled completely to the top, then put the lid back on. Be careful not to turn the jars upside down or shake them once the resident is finished. If the sand reaches the lid, the design will be stable for the most part, but the sand can still shift a little and alter the resident's creation.

Variation: Colored Rice. This can also be done by layering colored rice. Add about ten drops of food coloring to two cups uncooked white rice and mix until you have the desired color. Any size jar will work with this activity.

Variation: Dried Beans. You can also make some colorful bean layers using different kinds of dried beans such as lentils, kidney beans, peas, lima beans, white navy beans, black-eyed peas or other colorful beans. Larger jars, such as mayonnaise jars, pint-size or quart-size canning jars work best with this activity. This activity can make a nice gift for the residents to give to friends or relatives if you add a recipe for bean soup with it.

Variation: Pasta Sampler. Use macaroni and pretty pastas in different colors as part of the layers. Quart-size canning jars or other larger jars work best with this activity. This makes a nice gift, too!

Designing with Sand

Materials Needed: Poster board or cardboard; glue; plain sand or different colors of sand; pen or pencil; shirt box.

Have your residents put their poster board in a shirt box or on a cafeteria tray and then draw a design or a picture on the poster board with the pen. They can then trace or cover a part of the design with glue and then sprinkle sand over it. After a few minutes the excess sand can be shaken off the poster board into the box or onto the tray.

Variation: Rice Designs. This same idea can be done with uncooked white rice by dyeing it with food coloring and using it in place of the sand. Rice can be colored by adding about ten drops of food coloring to two cups of uncooked white rice and mixing.

Spring Garden

Materials Needed: Potting soil; seeds; a variety of cut flowers with ends wrapped in wet paper towels or standing in a can of water; 2–3 small pots or plastic cups per resident; scoops; a pitcher of water; magazine pictures or photographs of wildflowers, flower arranging and/or flower gardens.

Place the cut flowers in the center of the table. Show the pictures of wild flowers and flower gardens to the residents to encourage conversation about flowers. Begin to talk about the shapes, smells and colors of the cut flowers—a great conversation starter.

Give the residents small cups about half-full of water to arrange several cut flowers. Watch how creative they can be.

Next you can have the residents plant seeds in another cup. Let them do it! The mess can be cleaned up later. Once the seeds are planted, the residents can set them in front of a window in their room, or put their name on the cup to water them in the activity room.

Spring Baskets

Materials Needed: Straw or wicker baskets; an assortment of silk or dried flowers; ribbon (optional).

Using dried or silk flowers, the residents can arrange flowers in straw or wicker baskets to use as centerpieces or spring decorations around the facility. The ribbon can be used to add an extra splash of color.

Spring Promise

This activity starts in the autumn, but finishes in the spring.

Materials Needed: Flower bulbs (such as tulips, daffodils, crocuses); a prepared plot of ground to plant the bulbs; trowels or bulb planters; refreshments; flower box or large planter and soil (optional).

Note: If you don't have a small gardening plot available or it is too cold outside for the residents, flower boxes or large planters can be substituted. If you choose to use planters don't forget to bring dirt or potting soil to fill them.

Go to a nursery and purchase several different kinds of flower bulbs such as tulips, daffodils, and crocuses. Spend time with a group of residents planting the bulbs in the ground or in flower boxes outside. If it is too chilly to go outside to do the actual planting, you might consider planting the bulbs in large pots which you can later move outside. The bulbs should be planted about eight inches underground with the pointed side of the bulb up, but check the package for recommended planting depth and spacing. Make sure you leave the bulbs outside during the winter months because they require the cold winter air in order to bloom in the spring. After this autumn activity serve hot cider, coffee, tea or hot chocolate. Just wait for springtime!

Even though the residents who planted the bulbs may not remember that they did so, there is still something exciting about watching a plant grow or a flower bloom.

Celebrate the first bloom with a Spring Party of lemonade and cookies.

Terrarium Art

Terrariums offer another opportunity to create with plants. Let your residents create their own "living landscapes."

Note: If you cannot find one of the suggested terrariums below, a clear, three-liter soda bottle with a black base can also be used. Cut off the spout, remove the black base, turn the bottle over and fit it down into the black base. The base will hold the dirt.

Materials Needed: Glass aquarium, fishbowl or see-through plastic cake box for the terrarium; plants such as ivies, ferns or mosses; fish tank gravel; potting soil; a spray bottle of water.

Have residents place ½ inch of gravel in the bottom of the container and then add about three inches of dirt over the gravel. Place each plant into the soil and then spray lightly with water. The terrarium should be covered with a sheet of glass, aluminum foil or plastic wrap. If using the soda bottle, the turned-over bottle acts as the lid. The terrarium can now be placed in a resident's window to enjoy. It shouldn't need any care since the moisture is trapped inside and it gets enough sunlight in the window.

Desert terrariums can also be made using sand mixed with potting soil and different kinds of cacti.

You may even want to create terrariums that represent plants from different parts of the world. These are interesting and can be educational as well. Talk about the types of climate necessary for different plants to grow.

Pebble Towers

Materials Needed: Smooth pebbles; white glue; aluminum pie tins; spray paint; varnish; Easter egg dye or food coloring (optional).

Have your residents squirt a layer of glue into the pie tin and place a layer of pebbles on the glue. Let this dry slightly before adding another layer of pebbles. Repeat these steps until a tower is built. When it is complete and the glue is dry, the tower can be spray painted, or varnished if the resident prefers a glossy finish.

Variation: Rainbow Rock Towers. Add another step to this activity by having the residents dye light-colored rocks before creating with them. This can be done with Easter egg dye or food coloring. Let the rocks dry before building with them.

Variation: Decorative Rock Creations. Use decorative garden rocks found at your local nursery.

Sun Prints

Materials Needed: Leaves; colored construction paper; straight pins or small rocks; *bright* sunshine.

Pin the leaves to colored paper or weigh them down with rocks. The rocks should not extend over the edge of the leaf. Place in the sunshine for about an hour and enjoy some refreshments! After an hour remove the leaves and a silhouette of the leaf will be left.

Sun prints can also be made of cardboard shapes, tools such as hammers or wrenches, kitchen utensils, and other opaque objects.

Arctic Rock Garden

It's a snow garden! It's easy to do and fun!

Caution: *The ingredients in this activity should not be placed in one's mouth or ingested. If you have a resident that puts things in his or her mouth, avoid this activity.*

Materials Needed: Small rocks which have been rinsed thoroughly; aluminum pie tins; four tablespoons salt; four tablespoons liquid bluing and four tablespoons water mixed together; one tablespoon ammonia; food coloring (optional).

Have a resident stir and dissolve the salt in the water and bluing as best he or she can. Add ammonia. Stir the mixture and then pour it slowly over rocks, covering all surfaces. The garden will begin to grow in a few hours. A few drops of food coloring may be added to the solution if a more colorful garden is desired.

Creating a Crystal Garden

This is an activity done primarily by the activity director and does require supervision, but allow the residents to participate in the preparation as much as possible.

Caution: *The ingredients in this activity should not be placed in one's mouth or ingested. If you have a resident that puts things in his or her mouth, avoid this activity.*
The briquettes can be messy and the liquid bluing and ammonia can irritate eyes and skin.

Prepare Ahead: Make the salt solution by mixing ¼ cup salt, ¼ cup liquid bluing and ¼ cup ammonia. Place it in a jar with a secure lid for later use.

Materials Needed: Six charcoal briquettes; food coloring; aluminum pie tin; salt solution; paper and pencils (optional).

Have the residents squeeze several drops of various colors of food coloring on each briquette. While supervised, they can then pour a few teaspoons of the salt solution on each briquette, and set the pan in a warm place. Keep the remainder of the solution in a jar with a secure lid for later use.

The residents can observe the growth of the crystals on the briquettes. More solution can be added to the garden every two days to keep the crystals growing. Have paper and pencils available because some of the residents may even want to keep a chart of the changes in the crystals.

Eggshell Pictures

Materials Needed: Save the eggshells from dyed Easter eggs and break them into small pieces (keep each color in a separate container); paper; glue.

The residents can squirt glue on the paper in any design they want. Then have them press the dyed eggshells into the glue to make colorful designs.

Printing with Leaves

Prepare Ahead: Take a nature walk and have the residents help collect different shapes and sizes of leaves.

Materials Needed: Tempera paint in autumn-leaf colors; water; white or Manila paper; paint brushes; any kind of extra paper (may be scrap).

Prepare the paint by mixing ½ cup liquid tempera with one teaspoon water, or one cup dry tempera paint with ⅓ cup water.

Show the residents how to paint the bottom (vein side) of the leaves and then place the painted side of the leaf down on the piece of paper. Have the residents place a piece of paper over the leaves and then rub their hands over the paper. Then they can lift the top paper and the leaf to reveal the print.

Variation: Wrapping paper or Notecards. The residents can use this technique to make their own wrapping paper or notecards. Just use large sheets of butcher paper for wrapping paper, or give the residents blank notecards to print with leaves instead.

Seed Mosaics

Materials Needed: A variety of seeds (popcorn, kidney beans, lima beans, pumpkin and sunflower, for example); glue; poster board or pieces of cardboard.

Place the different kinds of seeds in separate piles or in empty yogurt containers in the center of the table. Let the residents select and glue the seeds on the poster board to make seed designs and pictures.

Seaside Collage

Materials Needed: A large, flat piece of driftwood or a piece of board; smaller pieces of driftwood; shells; bits of dry seaweed; seagull feathers; rocks; glue.

Glue the seashore items to the large piece of wood to make a seaside collage. This can be done as a group or by an individual resident.

Autumn Table Decoration

Materials Needed: A medium-size basket; dried flowers (check at craft stores for donations); leaves; dried moss; gourds and small pumpkins.

Invite the residents to design an autumn table decoration. Let the residents be creative! This activity may be done individually or in a group.

Variations: Seasonal. You can modify this activity for any season or month of the year—use pine cones, holly leaves, pine tree clippings at Christmas, stuffed or plastic chicks and hard-boiled eggs in springtime, and so forth. Designing table centerpieces can be a monthly activity with a theme for each month.

Shucking Corn

Materials Needed: Country music, plastic to cover work area; unshucked corn; preheated crock pot with water added, butter and salt (optional).

Put on some good "old" country music, sit around a table or plastic laid out on the floor and have some fun with corn-husking time! Provide several unshucked ears of corn per resident and let them peel back the husk and the silk. This is a great tactile and olfactory stimulation activity. There are so many different textures, and fresh corn smells wonderful. Encourage reminiscence.

This activity only takes about ten minutes. Afterward, the corn can be used for Fruit and Vegetable Printmaking (page 23), or cook it for an old time snack. Rinse the corn off and put it in the crock pot with the heated water for about ten minutes. Serve with melted butter and a dash of salt. You may want to have a sharp knife available to cut the corn away from the cob and some plastic forks for the residents who can't eat the corn right off the cob.

You might even be able to find someone to demonstrate how to make a corn husk doll. Some of the more able residents may be able to do it themselves. See the description below.

Corn Husk Doll

Depending on the abilities of your residents, you may choose to do this activity, or have someone else demonstrate it for them. If you choose to demonstrate how to make corn husk dolls, encourage the residents to reminisce. Once complete, these dolls can be used as seasonal decorations, or as centerpieces.

Prepare Ahead: Save corn husks and silk. Dry them until they are a light straw color.

Once dried, sprinkle the husks with water and place in a plastic bag overnight so they will soften.

Materials Needed: Corn husks and silk from six or seven ears of corn; water; plastic bags; five-inch lengths of thin, pliable wire; heavy-duty beige thread; glue.

Roll five of the husks together lengthwise. Tie the center with thread. Peel the top half down and tie again one inch below the top to make a head.

Roll five more husks together lengthwise (same as above) and tie around the center. Set it on top of the first one, peel it over the first one and tie off. Wrap a ¼-inch strip of husk one inch below the top.

To make the arms, use one piece of husk. Weave the five-inch piece of wire through it and wrap the husk around the wire. Tie off in the center and at both ends (the wrists).

Tie ¼-inch wide pieces of husk strips around the wrists and elbows. Attach the arms to the body by lifting up part of the body husk and tie them on with ¼-inch wide pieces of husk. To do this the ¼-inch wide piece of husk should run from the left hip to the right shoulder, around the neck and down to the right hip and around the lower back. Tie in a knot. If your ¼-inch pieces of husk are too short, you can attach the arms with two ¼-inch wide pieces of husk in an X by running the ¼-inch wide pieces over opposite hips and shoulders and tying each of them off.

Next, cover these pieces with ¾-inch wide strips of husk. Tie another ¾-inch piece of husk around the waist.

Wrap layers of husks with the wide ends down around the waist to make a skirt and tie in place with beige thread. Hide the waist with ¾-inch wide piece of husk strip.

Glue corn silk on for hair and use a pen or marker to make the face.

1. Roll five husks together lengthwise. Tie the center with thread.

2. Peel the top half down and tie with thread one inch below the top to make a head.

3. Roll five more husks together and tie around the center.

4. Set it onto the head of the first one, peel it over and tie off with thread one inch below the top. Wrap ¼-inch strip of husk over the thread.

5. Make arms with one piece of husk by weaving a five-inch piece of wire through it then wrapping the husk around the wire. Tie off with thread at both ends to make the wrists.

   Tie ¼-inch wide pieces of husk strips around the wrists and elbows.

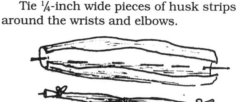

6. Attach the arms to the body by lifting up part of the body husk and placing the arms underneath a strip or two of body husk. Secure the arms with ¼-inch wide strips of husk by wrapping it in an X around the body. Tie of ends of ¼-inch wide strips.

7. Cover the ¼-inch wide strips of husk with ¾-inch wide strips of husk. Tie on with a ¼-inch wide strip of husk around the waist. Cover with a ¾-inch wide strip of husk.

8. Wrap layers of husks around the waist to make a skirt. Tie in place with thread.

9. Hide the waist with a ¾-inch wide strip of husk. Glue on corn silk for hair and use a pen or marker to

Chapter 8
Musical Expressions

Music is a wonderful tool. Use it with everything you do! Perhaps this quote has been uttered by you—"I really can't sing. I am tone deaf and have never played an instrument in my life. How can *I* possibly include music in my activities?"

You may need to be able to carry a tune for the opera or be proficient playing an instrument for the symphony, but *not* when using music with nursing home residents. Music has meaning for people of all ages. It is one of the best means of communication. Music promotes socialization. It is enjoyable. It increases a feeling of well-being. It exercises memory and increases attention span. Music invites active participation. Have you ever tried to sit through a certain song without tapping your toe? Music can also encourage relaxation. It usually has a great calming effect. Keep in mind that the music itself is more important than the words. But isn't it interesting how even residents with dementia can remember the words to old hymns?

Use music informally in the background, or as a motivator in another activity. Carry a small, portable tape player with you. Paint to it. Exercise to it. Use it formally in a scheduled music activity. Use music with your residents whenever possible.

Here are a few of the many activities you can do that involve music. Use these as a starting point for your own musical programs.

Musical Bottles

Try this activity when visiting residents in their room or in a group setting.

Materials Needed: Eight empty, glass soft drink bottles; a pitcher of water; a metal spoon; a funnel; a cafeteria tray for transporting these items to residents' rooms.

Let the resident pour different amounts of water into each bottle. Have him or her arrange the bottles in order from the one with the least amount of water to the one with the highest water level. Let him or her tap each bottle with the metal

spoon to hear the different sounds each bottle makes. Then see if the resident can play a song with the bottles using the metal spoon. Also if he or she is able, the resident can blow across the top of the bottles to hear the different sounds produced by each one.

Mirroring

Materials Needed: Music (classical or tunes that would be familiar to the residents); a tape/CD player.

Divide the residents into pairs. (The facilitator can be the partner of a room-bound resident.) Everyone should be able to face their partner. Put the music on. Old familiar tunes or classical music work best. Guide one resident to create different movements with his or her body while the other resident follows the motions as a mirror would do. Change roles halfway through the musical selection, or change roles several times. This is great exercise, a whole lot of fun, and can help increase use of the resident's concentration and attention span.

Hand Dancing

Materials Needed: Music (classical or tunes that would be familiar to the residents); a tape/CD player; glow-in-the-dark gloves (optional).

This activity also gives the residents the benefits of music and exercise. Choose music that has different tempos and have everyone dance with their hands and arms. You may be amazed at the number of possible expressions with hands and fingers. The residents can dance with their hands in the air, dance their hands across the tabletop, or dance their fingers over the bedspread.

To add a little variety to this activity, find some glow-in-the-dark gloves at a costume shop or theatrical supply store. Put on the gloves, turn off the lights and shut the drapes in the room. It's great fun and the glowing hands are delightful to watch as they dance around.

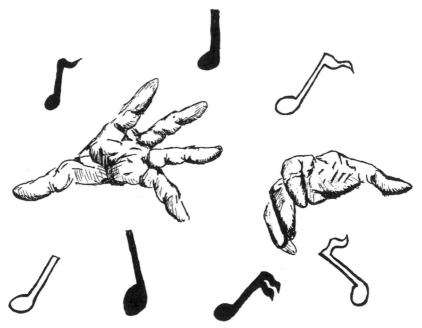

Variation: Toe Dancing. This is a great one-on-one activity to do with room-bound residents also. Let the residents take off their shoes and socks and toe dance to the music!

"Dance Along"

Materials Needed: Any music, any time, any place.

This is not a formal dance. The idea is to be spontaneous. A "dance along" can take place just about anywhere, anytime. Whether it is the music playing over the intercom system, someone is playing a piano, a tape or CD player is playing or even music from the television or VCR, it can be an opportunity for the residents to get up and dance. Remember, the residents will follow your lead. Maybe as they wait for a meal or activity, or when refreshments have been served after an activity, encourage the residents to dance. It can happen any time and any place! Many dementia residents who rarely respond to anything will smile and dance when given some music and a lead. Sometimes there may be only one resident who gets up to dance. That's OK. Encourage them all to "dance along."

Pass The Face

Prepare Ahead: (Optional) Cut faces with different expressions out of magazines ahead of time. Mount the pictures on construction paper.

Materials Needed: Music; prepared pictures of faces (optional).

Play some music and have the residents sit in a circle. Choose a resident to begin. Tell him or her to put an expression on his or her face and turn to the person next to them. Have the next resident "take off" their exaggerated expression and pass it to the resident next to them. This is a great interactive activity.

If it makes it easier to get started, you can use the faces with different expressions that you prepared earlier. Have the residents pass the pictures face down around the circle. When the music stops the resident must turn over the picture in hand and put that expression on his or her own face.

Variation: *Pass the Handshake.* This can be used as an opener for another activity. Put some music on, sit in a circle and begin by shaking hands with the resident next to you. That resident then turns to shake hands with the resident next to them. Continue around the circle until everyone gets a handshake.

Variation: Pass the Hug. This is the same idea as pass the handshake and a good opener before starting another activity also, just do it with hugs instead. Touch is often missing in nursing home environments.

Waving Colored Scarves

This is fun, and a great way to add variety to an exercise program.

Prepare Ahead: Make a tape of music that includes both lively and quiet selections. Start with slower tempos and increase the pace, then slow it down again. The music can be instrumental or include lyrics. When the music is familiar to the residents, they can sing along.

Materials Needed: A tape player; prepared tape; a variety of colorful scarves, streamers or strips of material.

Provide colorful scarves or streamers made from scraps of leftover material (material may be donated). Use a wide variety of bright colors if possible.

Play the prepared tape and encourage the residents to move the scarves to the music. Encourage as many different ways of movement as possible. Have the residents listen to the tempo of the musical selections from a tape of both quiet and lively music and move their streamers accordingly. Some residents may even get up and dance!

Musical Parachute

Prepare Ahead: If you cannot find a parachute, purchase two colorful nonfitted bedsheets. These can then be sewn together to get the same effect as a parachute.

Materials Needed: A colorful parachute (or two colorful top sheets sewn together); music; seasonal cutouts made of construction paper (optional).

Colorful parachutes can be purchased through many activity and therapeutic recreation catalogs. If you don't have one, or would like to try a more economic alternative, a colorful bedsheet will work fine (see Prepare Ahead).

Choose musical selections with different tempos. Have the residents sit in a circle and grasp the edge of the parachute. As the music plays the residents can move their arms up and down either slowly or quickly.

Variation: Seasonal. Add some seasonal fun by putting 50–100 construction paper leaves in fall colors to the middle of the parachute that will look like falling leaves as the parachute moves. Other ideas include red cutout hearts for Valentine's Day; colorful flowers for spring; snowflakes for winter; red, white and blue stars for the Fourth of July, or whatever else you can think of—be creative.

Musical Balloons

Materials Needed: Colorful balloons (one for each pair of residents; 2–3 for circle groups); music.

This is similar to a favorite game called balloon volleyball. Just add music! As the music plays, the residents can sit in a circle or line up across from each other and hit the balloons back and forth to each other. Use several colors of balloons.

The residents have so much fun they don't even think about the benefits of exercise!

This activity can also be done in pairs with the facilitator and a room-bound resident or a resident sitting in a lobby or hall.

Relaxing Bubbles

Materials Needed: Music; bubble solution; bubble wands.

This is a great activity to do with several young volunteers. Play some relaxing music while volunteers blow bubbles using various sizes of bubble wands. There is something very relaxing about watching bubbles. This can be done with large groups as well as in a resident's room.

Music and Mime

Materials Needed: Music (and imagination!)

This can be done from a wheelchair, chair, bed, or standing up. Play gentle background music and have your residents follow some of these directions:

- Pretend you are floating like a kite.
- Pretend you are riding in a hot air balloon and a gentle breeze is blowing.
- Pretend you are holding a balloon that is pulling you upward into the sky.
- Pretend you are a snowflake in a snowstorm.
- Pretend you are a flower blooming.

Play livelier music and have your residents follow some of these directions:

- Pretend you are bacon sizzling.
- Pretend you are popcorn popping.
- Pretend you are a humming bird.
- Pretend you are a balloon that someone just let the air out of.

Make up some of your own. It's great fun!

Rhythm Band

Prepare Ahead: (This can be a separate activity involving residents who are able.) Construct rhythm band instruments. Glue sandpaper onto blocks to rub together. Cover empty boxes with contact paper and fill with beans to shake. Sew jingle bells onto a piece of cloth to shake. Make tambourines out of heavy cardboard plates. Just about anything that makes noise can be an instrument.

Materials Needed: Rhythm band instruments.

This is an old favorite in nursing homes. Most of the time it is thought of as just another activity to put on the calendar. But consider the therapeutic value and the opportunity to create. Try putting a rhythm band instrument into the hands of a resident. Rhythm band instruments can be purchased but they can be easily made. Put on some music and let the residents play along.

Variation: Kitchen Band. A kitchen band can be made with pots and pans, spoons, washboards, or almost anything else you can find in a kitchen.

Musical Grab Bag

If using instruments that require mouth contact (such as recorders), add rubbing alcohol to your Materials Needed list so that the mouthpieces can be cleaned between players.

Materials Needed: A large cloth laundry bag or covered box; instruments; music.

Use a large cloth duffel bag, or even a covered box, and fill it with different rhythm band instruments. Let each resident take turns grabbing an instrument from the bag and then playing the instrument.

This will start as a solo and end up as a band if there are enough instruments for each resident.

Variation: Pass and Play. Play some music and have a resident grab an instrument from the bag and play along with the music. When they are through, they put the instrument back in the bag and pass it to the next resident. That resident removes an instrument from the garb bag and does the same.

Variation: Songwriters' Grab Bag. A variation to this, which is also fun, is to fill the bag with different objects such as a shoe, a flower, a brush, or any other objects available. When a resident draws an object out of the bag they can make up a song about the object they drew.

Song Dice

Prepare Ahead: Make cubes out of cloth and stuff them so they look like dice, or use a large wooden or plastic cube. This is a good project for a volunteer. On each side of the cube write the title of a favorite old song or hymn. When you're finished you will have "song dice." Make as many as you'd like with different songs on each one.

If your facility has large-print songbooks available, you may want to use it as a resource to make the dice and have the songbook available for the activity, but it's not necessary.

Materials Needed: Song dice; song books and accompanist (optional).

Sit in a circle and let the residents take turns throwing one of the song dice. Whichever song is facing up is the one for the group to sing. This has always been a fun activity which brings a lot of laughter—especially when the same song shows up more than once!

As long as the song dice use tunes familiar to the residents, a songbook won't be necessary. If you can find a volunteer accompanist, this would be a good activity to do with them.

Musical Suitcase

Materials Needed: A small suitcase the residents can pass around to each other; an assortment of hats, scarves and ties; music.

Fill a small suitcase with several different hats, scarves or ties. As the music plays have the residents pass the suitcase around the circle. When you turn off the music, the resident holding the suitcase takes out a scarf or hat, puts it on and leads the group in a favorite song. This adds spice to a sing-along activity.

Musical Chairs

Materials Needed: Music; chairs or a "hot potato" item.

This is an old game that people often associate with children, but I've seen many adults that absolutely love this activity! Put a few chairs in a circle (one less than the number of residents) and put some music on. The residents will march around the circle of chairs until the music stops. The resident left without a chair is out. If you have one or more participants who use wheelchairs, this activity can still be played by using a "hot potato." The residents pass around the "potato" as the music plays. The resident left holding the "hot potato" when the music stops is out.

Xylophone

This can be done alone or with a group.

Materials Needed: A xylophone or autoharp.

These instruments make a nice sound and can give a resident the opportunity to create music while they are sitting in a chair or in bed. Both are fun to play and make beautiful music.

Silly Songs

Materials Needed: None, but you many be able to find instrumental versions of familiar tunes to
sing the final compositions.

Although you may never make a record, songwriting is great
fun. Ever heard of "piggyback songs?" They are simply
songs that have been made up by taking a familiar tune and
creating new words. For example, tell your residents to hum
the song "Twinkle, Twinkle Little Star." Then, using the
same tune, have them write their own words—

> Nurses come to give us meds,
> Housekeeping always makes our beds,
> The nurse's aides are always here,
> Activity directors bring us cheer.
> Living here is pretty swell,
> In fact I like it pretty well.

Musical Socks

This is an activity that can offer opportunity for residents
who wander or are agitated to take part in a constructive
activity.

Materials Needed: Music; socks to sort and fold or washcloths to fold; a large plastic laundry
basket.

Get a large, plastic laundry basket with many pairs of socks
in different colors. Play some music and show the resident
how to begin matching and folding the socks. This may keep
them occupied longer than you think!

You can also get several colored washcloths and put them
in a pile for a resident to fold while music is playing.

Wind Chimes

Materials Needed: Wind chimes; ceiling hooks (optional).

There's something quite soothing and relaxing about wind chimes. Hang some outside on the porch and let the residents sit outside and listen to the beautiful music created by the wind.

For room-bound residents, you can hang wind chimes outside their window or carry a small wind chime from room to room while visiting.

Variation: Music Boxes. You can also carry music boxes to the residents' rooms. Sometimes you can find a volunteer who collects music boxes that can bring a different one each week to talk about and play for the residents.

Chapter 9

Creative Expressions

Here are just a few ideas to get you started. Nursing home residents can be some of the most creative, expressive people you can meet when given the opportunity. Don't say, "My residents will never do this!" Give them an opportunity. You might be surprised. Let them embrace imagination freely! But first, you must embrace your own imagination.

This chapter falls into the category of theater arts. Theater arts can include just about anything when the residents are given the opportunity to assume or create a character role.

This chapter also includes creative storytelling, poetry reading or writing, and movement. There are opportunities for both verbal and nonverbal body expression and communication. Many of these ideas offer opportunities to stimulate social interaction. Some of these activities can be serious and some can be just plain silly. Everybody needs a little of both in their lives!

Try these activities in large groups, small groups and in one-on-one situations.

Abstract Puppets

This gives residents an opportunity to be creative in a few different ways—puppet making, playwriting, and performance.

Materials Needed: Pieces of poster board or cardboard; scissors; white glue; construction paper; buttons, sequins, fabric scraps, tongue depressors or anything else you have around.

Let each resident cut out any shape from a piece of poster board. (The facilitator may have to help with the cutting since some residents have a difficult time using scissors and sometimes it's not safe for residents to use scissors). Tell the residents that they will be creating "abstract" puppets meaning that the puppets don't have to look like anything in particular. Give the residents glue and an assortment of materials for designing their puppets. Remind them that their puppets don't have to "look" like anything. One puppet may be a raindrop or a snowflake. Another puppet could be an animal. Another puppet may be a flower and so on. It's amazing to see how creative your residents can be with this activity!

When they're finished making their puppets and while the glue is drying, have the residents work together to create and plan a show for their puppets.

Often you will discover that the residents find a brief alleviation from the sometimes harsh reality of their present situation by playing the role of another—even if it is just an abstract puppet.

Many More Puppets Ideas

Puppets have been great fun for centuries. Finger puppets can be made by drawing a face on fingertips, stick puppets can be made with tongue depressors. Everyone has seen sock puppets—what fun it is to dress up a sock! A garden glove can be turned into five little finger puppets. Puppets can be made out of just about anything.

Give your residents a chance to use their imaginations and create all sorts of characters. Encourage the residents to put on puppet show with their creations. If your residents are willing to put on a production, you can invite a local day-care center to enjoy the residents' efforts.

Scarecrow Creation

A fun and funny creative activity for fall! This activity can even spark conversation and reminiscence about *The Wizard of Oz*, gardening, farming or harvest time.

Materials Needed: Several newspapers; a pair of old blue jeans; on old shirt; a straw hat and a balloon or ball; music (background); permanent marker (to draw face).

While music is playing and reminiscing is taking place have the residents take sheets of newspaper and wad them into balls. They can throw them across the room to you or to another resident who is stuffing the scarecrow's clothes with the newspaper balls. When the clothes are stuffed and assembled, set the balloon (or ball) on top of the shirt and put a hat on it's head. Draw a face on the scarecrow and set it in a chair as a decoration during the autumn months. Great fun and lots of laughs.

Stuffed Pillows

Prepare Ahead: Make a pillow blank by sewing three sides of two 12-inch square pieces of material together. Use materials with variety of colors and textures. Some residents may even be able to help you with the preparation.

To do this, cut two 12x12-inch squares from a colorful fabric. Place the printed sides together. Sew three of the four sides together. Turn the pillow blank right side out (the pattern should be on the outside and the raw edges inside). Now the pillow is ready to be stuffed. Make enough for each resident.

Materials Needed: Pillow blanks for each resident; pillow stuffing; needles and thread to finish pillows once stuffed; some music or a reminiscence topic.

Residents will enjoy stuffing pillows. It's a great sensory stimulation activity and good movement. Some residents will even be able to finish sewing the pillows once they are stuffed. But the best part comes last. Try having a good old-fashioned pillow fight, or toss the pillows back and forth to some music. Sure is good for a few laughs!

Seaside Summer

This can be fun, relaxing, and can even encourage reminiscence for those residents who lived near the seaside or visited the beach while on vacation. Sand can be purchased from nurseries and at some retail stores and large toy stores.

Materials Needed: A wading pool; 50–100 pounds of sand; nature or seashore sounds tape; tape player; sea shells (optional).

Nature tapes of ocean and beach sounds can be played in the background. Fill the wading pool with sand. Have the residents sit in a circle around the pool of sand, take off their shoes, and wiggle their toes in the sand!

Variation: Traveling Seashore. This activity can be taken to room-bound residents. Fill a plastic dishpan with sand, put various seashells on the sand, and don't forget the beach sounds tape! Instead of their feet, they can run their hands through the sand.

Creating a Circle Story

Materials Needed: Tape recorder and blank tape (optional).

Have a group of residents sit in a circle. Choose someone to begin the story. Either the resident can make up his or her own beginning or you can get the group started on the story by deciding on a theme such as, "Once upon a time when I was walking down the country road after fishing all day, I spotted a giant _____." The idea is that the next person picks up where the first person stops. Anything goes! There's nothing right or wrong about the direction the story takes. As you go around the circle give each resident a chance to add to the story. There will probably be plenty of laughs. For even more fun you can record the story and play it back to them when it's done.

Variation: Circle Poetry. Try starting with a line of poetry instead. The next resident picks up where the last one left off. Each resident adds a line to the poem in turn. Remember, anything goes!

Illustrated Story

Prepare Ahead: Sort through magazines and find large pictures to tear out and mount on construction paper. The pictures don't have to be related at all.

Materials Needed: Mounted pictures.

During this activity have the residents sit in a circle. Place a picture face down on each resident's lap. Choose someone to begin the story. They can look at their picture and make up a short paragraph about the picture. When the first resident is finished the next resident looks at his or her picture and continues the first's story linking his or her picture to the previous story and picture.

Variation: Seasonal Stories. This can also be done for holidays or seasonal activities. For instance, cut out pictures having to do only with Christmas, the Fourth of July, or other holidays.

Group Poetry Creation

Materials Needed: Butcher paper; a bulletin board; tacks or tape; a large felt-tip marker; tape recorder and blank tape (optional); tablet and pen (variation only).

Put a large sheet of butcher paper on a bulletin board where everyone can see it. You may want to begin the poem with a line of your own. Something like, "Drops of water danced on the flower petals." Leave a felt-tip marker by the board or attached to the board with a piece of yarn so that residents can add a line to the poem whenever they choose. It's amazing how creative the residents will be! Don't be surprised if the staff gets involved too!

Variation: Room-visit Group Poetry. This can also be done while going room to room and letting residents add to the poem. It can either be recorded or written on a tablet. Let everyone who participated read the poem when it's done.

Shadow Dancing

Materials Needed: Bright sunshine or a bright light; a wall; music.

This can be done outside on a sunny day or by using a light on the wall inside. Most everyone has done this and it's great fun!

Just get your residents started making shadows with their hands or body. It's fun to see just what can be created. Don't forget the music!

Living Sculptures

Prepare Ahead: Write ideas for living sculptures on slips of paper. You may not need them, but it's good to have some ideas to draw out of a box or bag.

Materials Needed: Music; idea slips and grab bag (optional).

There are a couple of variations to this activity. Put some music on in the background for atmosphere. First you might want to try the "still pantomime" approach with the residents. Residents decide what their sculpture will be and then *they* become that sculpture. Encourage them to be very still. You may even want to write ideas for their sculptures on pieces of paper and have each resident draw the ideas out of a box or bag.

Variation: Sculpting Partners. Another way to do this creates opportunity for resident interaction and can be a lot of fun. Pair up your residents. One resident is the "sculptor" and the other resident is the "living sculpture." The sculptor begins to carefully move his partner's head, arms, shoulders, and so forth to form his or her work of art. Don't forget to put the background music on!

Around The World in 80 Days

Prepare Ahead: Make tags from Manila paper to attach to the balloons. Include the phone number of the facility and ask whoever finds it to call in and tell you where they found it.

Materials Needed: Helium-filled balloon; tags.

Many nursing homes do balloon launches. This is a balloon launch with a creative twist. You will need a helium-filled balloon for every resident. Instead of just releasing the balloon, have the residents create an "adventure" for his or her balloon. Go around the circle and have each resident share

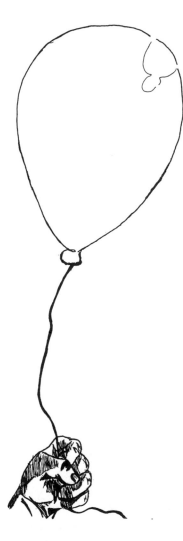

what will happen to his or her balloon after its release. It's amazing what great storytellers the residents can turn out to be.

Variation: Balloon Circle Story. Pass one balloon around from resident to resident and have the group create an adventure for the balloon using the 'circle story' method on page 124. Release the balloon afterward.

Create a Skit

Materials Needed: Assorted props such as scarves, ties, a purse, apron, a variety of hats, roll of toilet paper, a baby diaper, a book, an old telephone, gardening trowel, stuffed animals, tools or anything else you can think of; a grab bag.

You can do this with one group or several small groups. Put several objects in a box. You may want to label this your theater arts "prop" box. Have each group draw two or three objects out of the bag. (It's more fun if all the objects are unrelated.) Have the group create and act out a skit based on the objects each of them drawn from the bag. Stress creativity. Just listen to the laughter!

Variation: Create-a-Commercial. Another idea along these same line is to have your residents create a television commercial to try to sell the "product" they found in the bag.

Crazy Symphony

Materials Needed: A tape recorder with a blank tape.

Designate a conductor—either yourself or a resident. Have the conductor choose an environment such as a beach, city, farm, jungle, schoolyard, train station or whatever else the conductor pleases. The conductor asks each resident to think of a sound or noise which is associated with the conductor's chosen place. The conductor asks each person to make their noise individually and explains that as the conductor the resident must make his or her noise when the he or she points to them. The conductor can have the group play in unison, solo, fast, slow, soft, loud—just about any way he or she likes. Be sure to record this crazy symphony on a tape recorder. It's great fun!

Famous Friends

This can be fun and is a good interactive activity.

Prepare Ahead: Write names of famous people on slips of paper.

Materials Needed: Slips of paper with famous people's names on them; a container.

Tell the residents to think of a famous person they would like to pretend to be. You can suggest Presidents, leaders, actor and actresses, or any other well-known person of the past or present. If a resident doesn't want to think of their own or if it is hard for them, you can write characters down on slips of paper for them to draw out of a container. Tell everyone to "become" their famous person, and without saying who they are, they can begin to talk with other residents in the group while acting out their persona. See who can identify the most people. Great self-expression!

Variation: Fictional Friends. The same idea can be done with characters from television, cartoons, books or other popular media.

Going on a Trip

Materials Needed: None.

Maybe you remember playing the game "Grandma's Trunk." This is the same idea. It's not only an opportunity for creative expression, but it's a great memory stimulation activity.

Have a small group of residents sit in a circle. Have one resident begin by saying "I'm going on a trip and in my suitcase I'm going to pack *shoes*." The next resident will then say, "I'm going on a trip and in my suitcase I'm going to pack *shoes* and _____." Every resident chooses what they will pack but must first repeat what the others have packed. This can be quite fun.

What's For Dinner?

Materials Needed: None.

This is the same idea as "Going on a Trip" above, only you give the residents an opportunity to create a meal. "Tonight for dinner we are going to have *chicken*." The next resident continues the idea. What a menu they can create! They could even "act" out their piece of food!

Creative Writing

Materials Needed: Paper and pencils; tape recorders (for those who cannot write).

This does require a physical ability to write, but you could always try using a tape recorder or even have residents dictate their thoughts to someone else.

It's usually easier to get started if there is an "assignment." Try having them write about some of the ideas below.

> "If I could go to the moon..."
> "When I'm President of the United States..."
> "If I were a cat for a day..."
> "The day I took a wrong turn..."
> "If everything happened backwards..."
> "When the tractor began to fly..."
> "A day as a child..."

Create some of your own. The residents can write about anything they choose!

Creative Photography

Materials Needed: A camera, several rolls of 12 exposure film; ability to develop film (or a budget for it).

When was the last time your residents had the opportunity to use a camera? You really should try this one. Buy several rolls of 12-exposure film. One at a time each resident can have the opportunity to be "Photographer for the Day." Develop the film quickly and then display the resident's works of art. It's a lot of fun to see what each resident chooses to photograph.

Chapter 10
Expressions of Thought

Activities that offer opportunities to think and express thoughts definitely have a creative aspect to them. We've already seen many ideas in this book that require thinking, but I want to add just a few more. These can be a great ways to boost self-esteem, self-confidence, and many times learn something new.

As you will see, several of these activities will require residents who have the ability to communicate their thoughts. You will also note that the more you do, the easier it will become for some of the residents to express their thoughts.

Several of these activities also involve reminiscence, which is without a doubt one of the greatest activities you can do with your residents. Many of these ideas will be familiar to you, and you may even be doing some already. Great! Keep it up. Everybody needs to have opportunity to think, to bring one's thoughts into existence, and to express those thoughts to others.

Who's News

Materials Needed: Current newspapers or news magazines.

The facilitator can choose several articles to read to the group, or ask the residents who read the newspaper to prepare ahead of time.

Whether you select a local paper, a magazine or a national paper, gather your residents together to discuss who is making the news, what the news is, and their input into what is being discussed. Encourage each resident to express his or her opinion. You might even ask further questions such as "If you were is this person's position what would you do?" or "Why do think this is so newsworthy?"

Of course you can also do this with any current event. It doesn't have to be people.

The Family Home

Materials Needed: Pictures of new homes (both outside and the rooms inside).

This is another discussion-type activity. You might bring pictures of what new homes look like today. These can either be taken with a camera or cut out of ads in newspapers or magazines. Be sure to bring some pictures of the rooms inside the house.

Show the pictures to the residents and then ask the residents to talk about the differences between homes today and homes they remember. You can ask some of the following questions:

- Describe the house you lived in as a child.
- Did you have a yard? Trees? Flowers? A porch swing?
- Did you have your own room or did you have to share with someone?
- What did you have in your kitchen? Describe the stove your mother cooked on when you were little.
- How did you heat your home?
- Did you always have indoor plumbing?
- Did it get hot in the summer?

Variation: Other Topics. Other discussion topics which would be similar to this activity might include pictures of political candidates from the past as well as the present. Residents can discuss voting, candidates, and political issues. This could also lead into a discussion of changes they have seen over the years such as men's and women's fashions, civil liberties, technological breakthroughs, and medicine.

Another topic might be transportation. Bring pictures of as many modes of transportation as you can find. Ask some of the following questions to get your residents thinking:

- When did you get your first car? What kind was it?
- Who taught you to drive?
- Set up a model railroad.
- Describe a train trip you have taken.
- What did you think when the first man went into space?
- What kinds of transportation will there be in twenty years?

Money Matters

Materials Needed: Advertisements; catalogs; tablets or
notebooks and pens (see variations).

This can be a one-on-one activity or small discussion group.
Many of your residents either have their own income or have
some limited Medicaid dollars to spend each month. During
this group you might help residents decide how much money
they need to spend each month for personal items and how
to budget for those items. You can bring store ads and catalogs in so your residents can shop from their rooms.

When residents bring up needs and wants but don't have
the finances let this be a time for open discussion and be
sure to validate their desire to purchase these things even if
you see them as unnecessary. Through creative thinking,
the group might come up with a solution or alternative.

You may even want to reminisce within this group by
asking some of the following discussion questions:

- What did your father do for a living?
- Did you get an allowance as a child or did you
  have to earn your own spending money?
- When did you get your first paying job?
- What were some ways your family cut back to save
  money?
- What was it like living during the Great Depression?
- What could you buy for $1 when you were a child?

Variation: The Stock Market. Continuing along the money
theme you may have some residents who are interested in
following the stock market. They can do this through the
newspaper and television.

To allow for a little creative outlet, give the residents
"portfolio" notebooks and "$10,000" to invest. Let the resi-
dents pretend to buy and sell stocks and bonds. Have them
keep track of their "purchases" in the notebook. Each day
or week you get together they can discuss earnings and what
to buy and sell. At that time they can sell and buy other
stocks if they like. If you want to encourage competition, see
whose portfolio earned the most in a week, in a month, or
in three months.

Variation: "If I had a million dollars..." Save up all those catalogs and ads you get in the mail and collect a few more. Give each resident a tablet and a pen. At the top left hand side of the page have them write "$1,000,000." Give them a wide variety of magazines, catalogs, local real estate listings, automobile ads (don't forget the sporty models), furniture ads, Sunday classifieds and anything else that you can collect (old Sears catalogs work great). Even seed and gardening catalogs are fair game—they "buy" trees and plants they want to put on any real estate they "purchase." Let them bring in their own catalogs and advertisements if they'd like to share with the group. They can look through them to buy anything they want, but...

Inform them that they are only allowed to buy one of anything—one home, one car, one boat, one dream vacation, one toaster—and to keep track of their "purchases" in their notebook by writing down what they "buy" to the right of the amount it costs, and subtracting how much each item costs from their million dollars. If they see something they like better but already have one, they can sell back items for their original "purchase price."

This can be great fun and take quite a while to do. (You may want to give them a set time in which to spend their million dollars—one month, three months, six months.) See who can spend their million first, who thought about everything to put in their home, who bought the most things, and who had the most money left after getting everything they needed.

Health Matters

Materials Needed: None.

During this small group activity, the purpose is to give your residents the opportunity to talk about their health, express concerns over physical problems, and talk about how they feel. It is not as important for you to be able to explain their health concerns to them as it is for each resident to be able to express how they feel and for you to validate their feelings. This activity offers a wonderful opportunity for emotional outlet, too.

Have You Ever?

Prepare Ahead: Visual aids about leisure or work activities cut from magazines and mounted on construction paper.

This activity is another opportunity for your residents to recall past experiences. To make this just a little bit different you can use visual aids. Using magazines, cut out pictures of things such as a cruise ship on the ocean, an airplane or train, skiing down a mountain, hiking, planting or harvesting crops, or any other work or leisure activity.

Glue each picture onto a piece of colored construction paper. When your group comes together turn the pictures over on a table face down. Have a resident choose one as the discussion topic. Hold up the picture, show it to the group, and ask, "Have you ever...been on an ocean cruise, flown on an airplane, and so forth." Ask one question for each picture to encourage conversation. When the conversation ends have another resident choose another picture.

Book Review

Materials Needed: A book and a reader, or a prerecorded book.

Some of the residents still read on their own. Add group reading time or use audiotaped books. After completing a book give the residents an opportunity to review the book. What did they like about it? Who was their favorite character? Encourage the residents to ask their own questions.

This Is Your Staff!

Prepare Ahead: Choose 10–15 staff members the residents would know and gather facts about each one of them. Write clues down on index cards; make an answer key for yourself (optional).

Materials Needed: Information cards or sheets.

This is a game—can it ever be fun! It's similar to the game show "This Is Your Life." It requires preparation in advance. Choose about ten to fifteen staff members that the residents know and gather some facts about each one. At the beginning of the game give them a couple of facts about one of the staff members until someone guesses who that person is. This is not only a fun game, but it helps the residents get to know the people who work with them just a little bit better.

Games Galore!

Materials Needed: Assorted games such as Boggle, Trivial Pursuit, MasterMind, Monopoly, Scrabble, Cribbage.

Games are fun, and they can often be educational and require a lot of thinking. Introduce the residents to games. They'll love them.

You can take just about any television game show and adapt it to your residents' abilities and the resources you have available. Some examples are "The Price is Right," "Wheel of Fortune," and "Jeopardy!" There are also many great trivia games that can be purchased from catalogs or found in toy stores.

A Christmas Affair

Materials Needed: None.

Why should *you* do all the work? If you're going to have a resident-centered program then the residents should have input. Let your residents get involved in the creative planning of the Christmas activities. Let them decide on decorations, and plan parties and menus. Give them the opportunity to decide how to celebrate Christmas each year. You can do this for any activity. Give them ownership of the program!

What Did They Say?

Prepare Ahead: Compile a collection of adages. There are many books available as resources for this. Place them on index cards for easy reference.

Materials Needed: A collection of adages.

As you sit in a group, read the first part of the adage and see if the residents can finish it. You'd be surprised how good they are at this. Here are a some examples:
- "A penny saved is...   *a penny earned.*"
- "All work and no play... *makes Jack a dull boy.*"
- "Too many cooks...   *spoil the broth.*"
- "Do unto others...   *as you would have others do unto you.*"

Pen Pals

Materials Needed: Stationery; pens or pencils; envelopes; postage.

This is the traditional idea of exchanging letters with someone. Residents can become pen pals with residents from other nursing facilities, other parts of the world, or even another part of their building. This is especially beneficial to those residents who are unable to leave their room much and it gives the resident an opportunity to share their thoughts in writing. Everyone enjoys getting mail!

If you have residents who cannot see or write very well you can have them dictate letters to a volunteer, family member or even another resident. You might even try having "Cassette Pals" instead of Pen Pals for residents who would rather record their letters. If you want to get more sophisticated try videotaping a resident's conversation and sending it to their pal, but make sure the recipient has access to a VCR first.

Strength Bombardment

Materials Needed: None.

This activity builds self-esteem. Have the residents sit in a circle with a chair in the center of the circle. One resident sits in the center of the circle while the other residents "bombard" him or her with all the strengths they see in that person. The resident in the center must remain silent until everyone is finished with their "bombarding." When everyone has had a turn let the resident in the center share how it feels to be so loved!

Pass the Bowl

Prepare Ahead: Make slips of paper with descriptions of personal landmarks such as: "My most embarrassing moment," "The best day of my life," "My worst day," "My greatest accomplishment."

Materials Needed: Prepared slips of paper (folded); a bowl.

Put pieces of paper into a bowl. Pass the bowl and have each resident draw a piece of paper and honestly tell the group how they felt during those moments.

Thoughts-Go-Round

Prepare Ahead: Cut out a circular piece of paper (about eight inches wide) for each participant. This can be done easily with a standard 8 ½ x 11-inch sheet of paper.

Materials Needed: Circular pieces of paper for each participant; pens or pencils.

Another great self-esteem builder. Have the residents sit around a table and give each person a round sheet of paper and a pencil or pen. Have them write *their* name in the center of the paper. Next have everyone pass their paper to the left, and each person writes what they appreciate about the person whose name is written in the center on the circle. Keep passing the papers until they come back to the original resident. Now read them aloud!

Great Americans

Materials Needed: None.

When this activity is over each person should feel like a "great American." Begin the group by discussing some great Americans and what they have done. Some people to begin with might be Betsy Ross, Thomas Jefferson, Davy Crockett, Abraham Lincoln, Harriet Tubman, Clara Barton, Mark Twain, Harriet Beecher Stowe, George Washington Carver, Elizabeth Cady Stanton, Helen Keller, Martin Luther King, Jr. or Mahalia Jackson.

After talking about the great things these people did ask your residents, "If you could do something great today, what would it be?" Ask them to tell about one great thing they have already done in their lives.

Mystery Person of the Day

This activity is especially good for residents who are mobile and need a challenge.

Prepare Ahead: Research a staff familiar to the residents and write (or type) clues about him or her on a sheet of paper.

Materials Needed: A bulletin board; prepared clue sheet.

You will need a bulletin board in a location that is accessible to the residents. Each day you will choose a staff member and, without naming that person, you will write clues on a piece of paper and post it where the residents can read it. The residents then try to guess who the staff person is.

Post the mystery person's name at the end of the day, or the next morning when you post the clues for the new mystery person.

Staff Scavenger Hunt

Materials Needed: Prepared clue sheet; pencils or pens.

Using this same idea as above, you can involve the residents in a scavenger hunt that will not only keep them mobile and thinking, but will promote social interaction. Give them a list of things they will need to find out. Some examples are: Find a staff person who has a birthday in July. Find a staff person who speaks two languages. Find a staff person wearing black shoes And so on and so on. The residents can write the names down on a piece of paper and turn them in at the end of the day.

You could add an incentive such as having refreshments with an administrator, spotlight the resident on the bulletin board, have cookies and punch with the staff or let them host a small social gathering with refreshments.

Administrator for the Day

Materials Needed: None.

Do you hear complaints often? Do residents have the opportunity to share concerns about the facility? Possibly you should let them help resolve some of these problems. Creative problem solving is good for all of us. Let the residents discuss the problems or concerns they have and then brainstorm solutions. They may have some good answers, but if nothing else, a better understanding and communication will open up between residents and administration.

Recipe Recall

Your purpose here is not necessarily to make a cookbook, but you will probably want to try some of the residents' recipes.

Materials Needed: Paper and pencils.

Whether you've realized it or not, many of your residents were once great cooks. And most of them probably still have those recipes in their head. What fun and what opportunity for expression to have your residents sit down together for a "recipe recall." When it comes to some of the favorites, like apple pie, you may even find some strong disagreements over the "best" or the "right" way to make it. That's part of the fun. When it's all over (and it could involve weeks of discussions) you will have a great collection of recipes. And what do you do with a great collection of recipes? Creative cooking, of course. See Cooking Expressions (Chapter 11) for more ideas on creative food activities.

Variation: Facility Cookbook. If you have a computer with a word processing program and a resident or two who love working with computers, why not suggest that the residents compile a facility cookbook? Many churches and non-profit groups do this sort of activity as a fundraiser. The final cookbook can also make great gifts for family and friends. Check with local copy shops about donating their services to print and bind the book.

Scientific Wonders

One of the great needs and challenges we have as people is being able to predict the outcome of events. After careful thought and expression of that thought, we can then take the opportunity to carry out our "experiments."

The residents need this type of a challenge as well. Give them opportunity to carefully consider what *could* happen and why, and then discuss it. Then let them find out if their predictions are correct. This can be very educational for all.

Here are a couple of ideas you might try using water.

Dissolving Facts

Materials Needed: A clear jar for each substance you wish to test; water; substances to test (see suggestions below); a spoon; prediction charts and pencils (optional).

Bring several clear jars of water to the table. Set them on a tray in the center of the table. Bring small amounts of a variety of materials such as sand, dirt, salt, flour, sugar, pepper, oil, cinnamon, peanut butter or anything else you have available that may or may not dissolve in water. Try to find some of the new packing peanuts that look like styrofoam but are made of corn starch; they dissolve in water.

Ask your residents what will happen when a material is added to the water. Will it dissolve? Will it settle to the bottom? Will it clump up? Consider each material one at a time. You may even want to have the residents record their predictions on a chart. Next you can place each item in its own jar of water and see what happens. Let each resident take an opportunity to add a material to water. It's interesting and definitely promotes expression of thought.

Does it Float?

This is similar to the previous activity.

Prepare Ahead: Ask residents to bring two or three items to test for floatability.

Materials Needed: A pan or tub of water; items to test (see suggestions below); prediction charts and pencils (optional).

The challenge here is to predict whether certain materials will float in water or sink to the bottom of the container. Instead of several separate jars of water you can use one tub or pan of water. Bring items such as paper clips, tongue depressors, medicine cups, leaves, rocks, Styrofoam pieces, keys, combs, and anything else you can find. Let your residents be responsible for bringing two or three things to try. Now they can predict whether the items will float or sink. Some of the results may surprise them.

Magnet Miracles

The same type of activity as the one above, but this time magnets are used instead of water.

Materials Needed: Magnets (various strengths); items to test (see suggestions below); prediction sheets and pencils (optional).

Collect as many items as you can such as pencils, jewelry, paper clips, safety pins, keys, paper, aluminum cans, nails, pieces of foil, tongue depressors, and other small items. Let the residents predict which items the magnets pick up and why. Next you can test their predictions. Magnets can be a lot of fun.

Chapter 11

Cooking Expressions

Most of your residents grew up cooking and baking. Many times it was a family activity. The gathering place for many families is the kitchen. There is something warm, comfortable and secure about the kitchen. For people from farming communities the harvest was never allowed to go to waste!

Cooking is a wonderful expression of different cultures and regions of the world. In most nursing facilities, however, cooking is done for the residents and there is no real opportunity for them to prepare a meal, a snack, or even provide refreshments for a party.

Cooking or preparing food in a group setting will not only offer the residents a wonderful opportunity to create, but will also encourage social interaction, conversation, and working together toward a common goal. There will usually be a few laughs as well. Obvious benefits are sensory stimulation, reminiscence, exercise, and the use of fine motor skills. Maybe the residents can prepare a luncheon for the staff, or plan and prepare a party for children from a local school or daycare center.

Don't limit these ideas to groups only. Most cooking activities can be adapted for a one-on-one setting in a resident's room. These ideas do not include "recipes" as much as they offer "ideas." There are thousands of cookbooks available with recipes to try. Keep in mind that sometimes it's the *process, not the product.*

NOTE: There are no federal regulations which prohibit residents from being involved in cooking-related activities.

Residents **cannot** go into the facility kitchen, but food preparation can take place in the dining room, the activity room, a multipurpose room, or even a resident's room. Work with the food service staff to schedule a time that the staff can cook or bake what the residents prepare. There are many food-related activities that do not require cooking, and there are several appliances that can be used outside the kitchen with proper supervision.

PRECAUTIONS: Never leave hot appliances unattended. Residents should always be closely supervised. Only give knives and potato peelers to residents who are capable of using them safely. All residents should wash their hands immediately before food-related activities. Make sure all preparation surfaces have been thoroughly cleaned.

Some supplies or equipment you may want to have on hand for cooking activities include:
   a crock pot
   a wok
   an electric skillet
   a blender
   a food processor
   a toaster
   a toaster oven
   muffin tins
   an outdoor grill or hibachi
   potato peelers
   wooden spoons
   mixing bowls
   cutting boards
   measuring cups and spoons
   aprons
   butter knives for spreads
   a cheese grater
   a variety of cookbooks

Fruit and Vegetable Preparation

Your residents rarely have the opportunity to prepare food for cooking or eating. When done within a group setting, it's a wonderful reminiscence activity. Have the residents peel carrots or potatoes, shell peas, cut or chop vegetables and fruits such as celery, carrots, potatoes, broccoli, cauliflower, tomatoes, lettuce, apples, pears, oranges, bananas, strawberries, melons, and peaches. The facilitator can wash the fruits and vegetables before preparation. Make a salad, arrange a platter of fruits or vegetables for dipping, or prepare a yummy vegetable soup or stew that can be cooked in a crock pot.

Here are a couple easy to prepare fruit and vegetable dips to try with the residents.

Delicious Vegetable Dip

makes about 2 cups

Supplies Needed: Ingredients (listed below); mixing bowls; cheese grater; measuring cups and spoons; wooden spoons.

1 ½ cups cottage cheese	1 tablespoon lemon juice
¾ cup grated cheddar cheese	¾ teaspoon dill weed
6 tablespoons plain yogurt	sprinkle of garlic powder
6 tablespoons mayonnaise	

Residents can grate cheese, squeeze lemon and measure out the rest of the ingredients. In a bowl the residents can mix together the cottage cheese, grated cheese, yogurt, mayonnaise, lemon juice, and dill weed. Add the garlic powder. Stir well and it's ready for dipping!

Sweet Fruit Dip

makes one cup

Supplies Needed: Ingredients (listed below); measuring cups and spoons; mixing bowls; wooden spoons.

1 cup plain yogurt
¼ teaspoon cinnamon
1 teaspoon honey
2 tablespoons unsweetened, defrosted
    orange juice concentrate

Using a bowl and a wooden spoon the residents can mix all the ingredients together until well blended. It's ready for the fruit!

Building Sandwiches

There are great recipes in most cookbooks for sandwiches, but let the residents be creative!

Materials Needed: Dull knives for spreading condiments; paper plates; a variety of breads or crackers; lunch meats; cheeses; cheese spread; mayonnaise; mustard; sprouts; lettuce; sliced tomatoes. Of course all of these items are all optional; use whatever sandwich fixings are available.

Place all ingredients in the center of the table. Give each resident a paper plate and a knife. Invite the residents to create their own sandwiches, or have them prepare sandwiches for another group or a luncheon.

Frozen Fruit Creations

If you have access to a freezer, this is another way the residents can create with food.

Bananasicles

makes 6 servings

Materials Needed: Ingredients (listed below); mixing bowls; measuring cups and spoons; wooden spoons; butter knives; a plate or wax paper; access to a freezer.

3 tablespoons unsweetened cocoa	3 firm bananas
2 tablespoon honey	½ cup granola or wheat germ
½ teaspoon vanilla	6 Popsicle sticks
1 tablespoons milk	

Have the residents mix the cocoa, honey, vanilla and milk in a bowl. The residents can then peel the bananas and cut them in half crosswise. Stick a Popsicle stick into the thick end of each banana and roll each banana in the cocoa mixture. Sprinkle on the granola (or wheat germ). Place the coated bananas on a piece of wax paper or plate and place in a freezer for two hours before eating.

Banana Bites

makes 6 servings

Supplies Needed: Ingredients (listed below); a cookie sheet; wax paper; butter knives and forks; nut chopper (optional); measuring cups and spoons; mixing bowls; wooden spoons; a small bowl; a plate; access to a freezer.

3 bananas	2 tablespoon wheat germ
⅓ cup crushed peanuts	⅓ cup honey

Cover a cookie sheet with wax paper. Have the residents peel the bananas and cut them into bite-size slices (about one inch long). Crush the peanuts (if they were not purchased crushed). Mix the peanuts with the wheat germ; pour the mixture onto a plate. Place the honey in a small bowl. Dip each piece of banana in the honey then roll it in the nut mixture. Put the bananas on the prepared cookie sheet. Place the cookie sheet in the freezer for 1–2 hours. Eat while still frozen. Tastes like a banana ice cream treat!

Ice Cream Creations

The residents will love having the opportunity to make their own ice cream sundae or banana split. Put several flavors of ice cream on the table and allow them to choose. They may need help scooping the ice cream if it is very hard.

Include a variety of toppings such as fudge, chocolate syrup, butterscotch, caramel and strawberry. Sprinkles, chopped peanuts, and almonds are also favorites. Don't forget the whipped cream!

If you've never made homemade ice cream with the residents, give it a try! Here's a recipe to get you started.

Easy Homemade Ice Cream

Supplies Needed: Ingredients (listed below); measuring cups and spoons; a crank-style ice cream maker; crushed ice or snow; ice cream salt or rock salt. Don't forget the bowls and spoons for serving.

2 cans sweetened condensed milk
½ pint whipping cream
1 can evaporated milk
1 tablespoon vanilla
1 can chocolate syrup or 1 cup of seasonal fruit for
    flavoring (optional)
Milk to fill can (2% or whole)

Combine all of the above ingredients in a one-gallon ice cream freezer. Leave about three inches at the top of the can when adding the milk. Alternate packing ice (or snow) and ice cream salt around the freezer can; crank for about 30 minutes. Your residents will enjoy doing this. It will probably bring back a lot of memories and it is great exercise! After cranking, cover the freezer with a couple of towels and let it sit for about 20 minutes. Then it's ready to eat!

Blender Creations

Great things can be made with a blender. Try these recipes for milk shakes, coffee coolers, fruit smoothies, and even peanut butter! The residents can measure and pour the ingredients in the blender and push the button to give it a whirl. It's fun to watch and tastes great.

Here are a few blender recipes you may want to try:

Milk Shakes

makes 3–4 servings

Materials Needed: Ingredients (listed below); a blender; an ice cream scoop; cups for serving.

Ice cream
Fruit or syrup for flavoring (optional)
Milk

Fill the blender with any flavor ice cream. Add fruit or syrup if desired. Pour about 1 cup of milk over the ice cream and blend until desired thickness. Serve.

Coffee Cooler

makes 3–4 servings

Materials Needed: Ingredients (listed below); measuring cups and spoons; a blender; cups for serving.

1 cup strong coffee, chilled (regular or decaffeinated)
1 pint chocolate ice cream
1 teaspoon vanilla
$\frac{1}{2}$ teaspoon cinnamon
$\frac{1}{4}$ teaspoon salt

Have the residents pour the coffee into the blender, spoon in the ice cream, and add the remaining ingredients. Blend 10–15 seconds or until the mixture reaches the desired thickness. Serve.

Fruit Smoothie

makes 4 servings

Materials Needed: Ingredients (listed below); measuring cups; cups for serving.

1 banana
10 strawberries

1 cup orange juice
1 pint vanilla or lemon
 frozen yogurt

Have the residents peel bananas, and wash and remove stems from the strawberries then put them in the blender. Then they can add the orange juice and yogurt to the blender. Blend 10–15 seconds until smooth. Serve.

Homemade Peanut Butter

Materials Needed: Ingredients (listed below); a blender; measuring cups and spoons; crackers and bread, butter knives and plates for serving; an airtight container for storage.

2 cups dry roasted peanuts or salted shelled Spanish peanuts in a can
1 tablespoon salad oil (only if using dry roasted peanuts)

Have residents measure the ingredients and put them in the blender; blend until desired consistency.

Homemade peanut butter is never quite as smooth as store-bought peanut butter, but it sure is good! Spread it on crackers or bread right away, or put it in an airtight container and store it in the refrigerator.

Party Beverages

Give the residents an opportunity to make punch for the next social gathering or party at your facility. Here are some great recipes where the preparation is half the fun!

Red Berry Punch

serves 25

Materials Needed: Ingredients (listed below); a wooden spoon; punch bowl.

2 6-ounce cans defrosted pink lemonade concentrate
4 10-ounce packages of frozen strawberries or raspberries, thawed
4 28-ounce bottles ginger ale, chilled
ice cubes

Have the residents mix the undrained berries and lemonade concentrate in a punch bowl. Then *slowly* pour in the ginger ale and stir gently. Add ice and it's ready to serve.

Banana Punch

serves 50

Materials Needed: Ingredients (listed below); can opener; wooden spoons; knife (to cut lemons, or cut them in half before the activity); mixing bowls; fork (to mash bananas); a large plastic container; access to a freezer.

6 cups water
3 cups sugar
1 46-ounce can pineapple juice
1 12-ounce can defrosted orange juice concentrate, prepared as directed on label
juice of 2 lemons
5 bananas, mashed
3 quarts ginger ale (add just before serving)

Residents can dissolve sugar in the water and then mix all the rest of the ingredients together except the ginger ale.

Freeze in a plastic container; overnight works best. About two hours before serving, set outside the freezer until the mixture is slushy. Pour it in a punch bowl, and slowly add the ginger ale.

Spring Fruit Punch

serves 25

Materials Needed: Ingredients (listed below); a pitcher of water; wooden spoons; ice cream scoop; punch bowl.

2 6-ounce cans frozen pink lemonade concentrate, defrosted and prepared as directed on the label
1 64-ounce bottle cranberry juice
1 10-ounce box frozen strawberries
1 pint lemon or lime sherbet
1 quart ginger ale

Residents can mix the lemonade, cranberry juice and frozen strawberries in a punch bowl. Just before serving, add the sherbet and ginger ale.

Hot Spiced Tea Mix

This mix can be stored in an airtight container or jar, and can make an excellent gift for residents to give to family and friends with the directions for making it.

Materials Needed: Ingredients (listed below); mixing bowl; wooden spoon; funnel; airtight storage container or jar.

1 cup unsweetened instant tea mix
2 cups powdered orange drink mix (Tang or other orange breakfast drink)
1 teaspoon cinnamon
$\frac{1}{2}$ teaspoon allspice
1 6-ounce envelope sweetened lemonade mix
1 cup sugar

Residents can measure and mix all the ingredients together. Place in an airtight container for storage.

To make the hot tea, pour hot water into a mug and add three heaping teaspoons of the mix.

Skillet Creations

Precautions: *To ensure safety when using the skillet, it can be placed in a cardboard box which is slightly larger than the skillet and about the same height. This will prevent accidental burns. Never leave the skillet unattended.*

Many delicious and fun foods can be prepared using an electric skillet. Here are a few suggestions for a small group or individual activity: make grilled cheese sandwiches, pancakes, French toast, scrambled or fried eggs, applesauce, or easy doughnuts.

Applesauce

Materials Needed: Ingredients (listed below); an electric skillet; potato peeler and paring knives; measuring cups and spoons; bowls and spoons to serve.

6 apples, pared, cored and sliced
1 cup water
½ cup brown sugar
½ teaspoon cinnamon or 1 tablespoon of cinnamon red hots

Allow the residents to pare, core and slice the apples if it is safe for them to use a paring knife and potato peeler. Place apples and water in the skillet and heat to boiling using the 350°F setting. Reduce heat to a simmer and cook about ten more minutes or until the apples are tender. Stir in the remaining ingredients and cook a few minutes longer. Serve warm or cold.

Easy Doughnuts

Materials Needed: Canned biscuits (enough for each participant); cooking oil; cinnamon sugar; powdered sugar; tongs; paper towels; bowls for each of the sugars.

Heat the oil in the skillet until hot. Give each resident a biscuit and have them flatten it slightly and poke a hole in the center about the size of a thumb's width. The facilitator should place the dough in the hot oil cooking and fry the doughnuts for about 30 seconds on each side. Tongs should be used to turn the doughnuts and to remove them from the oil. Allow the doughnuts to drain for about a minute on a paper towel then place them in one of the bowls of sugar to cool. Quick and easy doughnuts are ready to serve!

Food Processor Fun

There are so many things you can do with a food processor. If you don't have a blender, a food processor can also blend ingredients.

Foods can be chopped grated, diced and sliced with a food processor with the right attachments. How about making French fries? They can be cut in less than a minute and then cooked in an electric skillet. Residents can grate cheese to melt over tortilla chips in the toaster oven to make nachos, or make a variety of slaws using cabbage, carrots or broccoli.

Toaster Oven Cooking

A toaster oven is the next best thing when you don't have a full-size oven available. You can bake cookies, muffins, brownies, cheese toast, cinnamon toast and even cook fish sticks and hot dogs. It gives the residents an opportunity to be involved in the "process."

Cookie Creations

Any of the old favorite recipes will do here—peanut butter cookies, chocolate chip cookies, sugar cookies, and snicker-doodles to name a few. The process will give your residents an opportunity to pour, measure, stir, knead, roll out, cut out, decorate, and (of course) eat! Cookies can be baked by the food service staff if it fits into their schedule, or they can be baked in a toaster oven by the residents.

You can also buy prepared dough in the refrigerator section of your grocery store that can be sliced, or rolled out and cut with cookie cutters. Decorating rolled out sugar cookies is a lot of fun. Provide residents with various cookie sprinkles to decorate before baking, or use frosting and sprinkles after the cookies have cooled.

Christmas is an excellent time to include cookie creations in an activity program.

Outdoor Creations

Nothing tastes better than hamburgers or hot dogs cooked outside on a grill or hibachi. Allow the residents to take part in an outdoor barbecue. You may even be able to roast marshmallows for dessert.

The potential recipes are endless for creative cooking with your residents. Allow the residents to remember old recipes and create new ones.

Afterword

Don't stop with just what you find in this book! After reading these ideas it will be your turn as an activity or recreation professional to be creative. Most activities can be adapted and changed to meet the needs and ability levels of almost all long-term care residents. Don't underestimate what the residents can do, or what they want to do. Remember, activities don't need to take a large budget.

Keep in mind that it is the *process* that is important, not the *product*. The greatest benefit comes while *doing* an activity. Don't be surprised if you see lasting benefits. Don't let it bother you if there is no finished product to show for the time spent in an activity. Give your residents the opportunity to create...*simple expressions.*

Other Books From Venture Publishing

Other Books From Venture Publishing

Interpretation of Cultural and Natural Resources
by Douglas M. Knudson, Ted T. Cable and Larry Beck

Introduction to Leisure Services—7th Edition
by H. Douglas Sessoms and Karla A. Henderson

Leadership and Administration of Outdoor Pursuits, Second Edition
by Phyllis Ford and James Blanchard

Leadership in Leisure Services: Making a Difference
by Debra J. Jordan

Leisure and Family Fun (LAFF)
by Mary Atteberry-Rogers

Leisure and Leisure Services in the 21st Century
by Geoffrey Godbey

The Leisure Diagnostic Battery: Users Manual and Sample Forms
by Peter A. Witt and Gary Ellis

Leisure Diagnostic Battery Computer Software
by Gary Ellis and Peter A. Witt

Leisure Education: A Manual of Activities and Resources
by Norma J. Stumbo and Steven R. Thompson

Leisure Education II: More Activities and Resources
by Norma J. Stumbo

Leisure Education III: More Goal-Oriented Activities
by Norma J. Stumbo

Leisure Education IV: Activities for Individuals With Substance Addictions
by Norma J. Stumbo

Leisure Education Program Planning: A Systematic Approach
by John Dattilo and William D. Murphy

Leisure in Your Life: An Exploration, Fourth Edition
by Geoffrey Godbey

Leisure Services in Canada: An Introduction
by Mark S. Searle and Russell E. Brayley

Leveraging the Benefits of Parks and Recreation: The Phoenix Project
by The California Park and Recreation Society

The Lifestory Re-Play Circle: A Manual of Activities and Techniques
by Rosilyn Wilder

More Than A Game: A New Focus on Senior Activity Services
by Brenda Corbett

Marketing for Parks, Recreation, and Leisure
by Ellen L. O'Sullivan

Models of Change in Municipal Parks and Recreation: A Book of Innovative Case Studies
edited by Mark E. Havitz

Nature and the Human Spirit: Toward an Expanded Land Management Ethic
edited by B. L. Driver, Daniel Dustin, Tony Baltic, Gary Elsner and George Peterson

Outdoor Recreation Management: Theory and Application, Third Edition
by Alan Jubenville and Ben Twight

Planning Parks for People, Second Edition
by John Hultsman, Richard L. Cottrell and Wendy Zales Hultsman

Private and Commercial Recreation
edited by Arlin Epperson

The Process of Recreation Programming Theory and Technique, Third Edition
by Patricia Farrell and Herberta M. Lundegren

Other Books From Venture Publishing

Protocols for Recreation Therapy Programs
edited by Jill Kelland, along with the
Recreation Therapy Staff at Alberta
Hospital Edmonton

*Quality Management: Applications for
Therapeutic Recreation*
edited by Bob Riley

*Recreation and Leisure: Issues in an Era
of Change, Third Edition*
edited by Thomas Goodale and Peter A.
Witt

*The Recreation Connection to Self-Esteem—
A Resource Manual for the Park, Recreation
and Community Services Professionals*
by The California Park and Recreation
Society

*Recreation Economic Decisions: Compar-
ing Benefits and Costs, Second Edition*
by John B. Loomis and Richard G.
Walsh

*Recreation Programming and Activities
for Older Adults*
by Jerold E. Elliott and Judith A. Sorg-
Elliott

*Recreation Programs That Work for
At-Risk Youth: The Challenge of Shaping
the Future*
edited by Peter A. Witt and John L.
Crompton

*Reference Manual for Writing Rehabilita-
tion Therapy Treatment Plans*
by Penny Hogberg and Mary Johnson

*Research in Therapeutic Recreation: Con-
cepts and Methods*
edited by Marjorie J. Malkin and
Christine Z. Howe

A Social History of Leisure Since 1600
by Gary Cross

A Social Psychology of Leisure
by Roger C. Mannell and Douglas A.
Kleiber

The Sociology of Leisure
by John R. Kelly and Geoffrey Godbey

*Therapeutic Activity Intervention with the
Elderly: Foundations and Practices*
by Barbara A. Hawkins, Marti E. May
and Nancy Brattain Rogers

*Therapeutic Recreation: Cases and
Exercises*
by Barbara C. Wilhite and M. Jean
Keller

Therapeutic Recreation in the Nursing Home
by Linda Buettner and Shelley L. Martin

*Therapeutic Recreation Protocol for
Treatment of Substance Addictions*
by Rozanne W. Faulkner

*Time for Life—The Surprising Ways
Americans Use Their Time*
by John P. Robinson and Geoffrey
Godbey

*A Training Manual for Americans With
Disabilities Act Compliance in Parks and
Recreation Settings*
by Carol Stensrud

*Understanding Leisure and Recreation:
Mapping the Past, Charting the Future*
edited by Edgar L. Jackson and Thomas
L. Burton

 Venture Publishing, Inc.
1999 Cato Avenue
State College, PA 16801

Phone: (814) 234-4561
Fax: (814) 234-1651
E-mail: vpublish@venturepublish.com
On the Web: www.venturepublish.com